In a Lifetime

From Hozier to U2

Johnny Lappin

Produced by Clare Keogh @EditingServices
Book Cover photography by Ibar Carty © Ibar Carty Collection
Book Cover design by Niall McCormack
Photographs © Ibar Carty/Johnny Lappin

ISBN-13: 9781796644036

Published by:
Foxrock Music Productions
Enniscorthy
Co Wexford
Republic of Ireland

DEDICATIONS

To George 'Ringo' Byrne and Richie 'Milkboy' Taylor, not forgetting 'Honest' Aiden Lambert, all of whom left us far too early.

In Memory of Dave Kavanagh 1956 - 2018

In a Lifetime - *From Hozier to U2*

TABLE OF CONTENTS

FOREWORD

I n March 1994 my late, great friend Richie 'Milkboy' Taylor, a musician who at the time was doubling as a music journalist for the Sunday Press, asked me to do an 'On The Couch' questionnaire for that paper. One of the questions he asked me was-

'Give us the five adjectives you believe best describe you.'-

'Gruff, rough, tough, charming and alarming.'

That was my immediate answer. Now, over thirty years later, I'm happy to say that I would probably give the same answer to the same question.

I've led an interesting, and to some, an unconventional life. I pride myself on the fact that I've never really had a *job* in my life, apart from one week working as a *gofer* in Dunnes Stores Supermarket in Cornelscourt in Dublin (circa 1967) which was short lived because I told my supervisor to rearrange the well-known two-word expression, ending in *off* because he asked me to follow a bizarre instruction that made absolutely no logical sense to me.

The other short-term job I had was in a factory in London as described in this book. I'm also discounting my years working in the family Painting & Decorating business which I still consider was a sentence rather than a job...

Music has been my life, and, as the fella said, if I had to do it again, I'd do it all over again! Counting it all up, I've spent more than fifty years working in, or around, the music business, and (I hope) I'm not finished yet. I've been asked so many times,

'How did you get into the music business?'

I've decided to write this missive in answer to that question and to set down this account before I've forgotten all the stories and characters I've encountered along the journey. I've been lucky, but as one famous professional golfer once said when asked about his luck, -

'The more I practice, the luckier I get'.

I know myself well and make no apologies for my forthright manner. I hate 'bullshit' and have always endeavoured to tell it like it is or was. Occasionally, my big mouth has gotten me into trouble, but I don't really care. I never went into the music business with popularity in mind.

Truth is the perfect disguise …

I hope you enjoy my story as much as I have living it!

Johnny Lappin

Chapter One

INTRODUCTION - THE HOZIER HIGH

I can remember the day very clearly. It was Monday, September 30, 2013. I had just returned from a week's holiday in Italy and hadn't yet got back into the usual round of meetings, phone-calls, demos to listen to and all the daily demands that are part of being a music publisher. Working from my home office in Enniscorthy in Co Wexford, I usually get up about 6am, feed my cats and make a coffee, then settle down to catch the TV news before moving into my office. I had nothing planned work-wise for this particular day, and after satisfying myself that the world hadn't ended, I switched on my computer to check my e-mails.

Holy Shit or more precisely *WTF* - I exclaimed to myself as my inbox filled with e-mails from London, New York & Los Angeles enquiring if I was the publisher to contact for Hozier's song 'Take Me To Church'. I'd just expected to see if I'd missed anything crucial while away before I started what I thought would be a relatively normal week. This deluge of e-mails threw me off completely, but I'd been around long enough to recognize something special had occurred for Hozier who was indeed signed to Evolving Music. This was extraordinary; it was not uncommon in the pre-digital era for record companies to descend en masse on the latest emergent talent. I remembered Ahmet Ertegun, boss of the legendary Atlantic Records, coming to Dublin in the 1980s with several other industry movers and shakers to check out An Emotional Fish in a small dingy Dublin pub, but I'd never witnessed a feeding frenzy like this in the new digital era.

I'd been working as a consultant to The Evolving Music Co Ltd, to give the company its full title, since 1994, an Irish music publishing company owned by Denis Desmond, the CEO of MCD, one of Ireland's top music promoters, and his wife Caroline Downey-Desmond.

The Evolving Music catalogue had initially included works by artists of the calibre of Jimmy MacCarthy and Sharon Shannon. Then, in 2007 we signed the duo Rodrigo y Gabriella, and the company shifted to a new level. But nothing to date had provoked the worldwide interest I now had to deal with regarding Hozier.

Evolving had signed Hozier to a worldwide publishing deal in 2010. Caroline had seen him perform in a school talent competition and had encouraged her husband Denis to sign him. His full name is Andrew Hozier-Byrne and he's from Newcastle in County Wicklow. His first release came out in July 2013 on the Rubyworks record label, a sister company of Evolving. It was an EP called 'Take Me to Church' that, alongside the title track, also included 'Like Real People Do', 'Angel of Small Death &The Codeine Scene' and 'Cherry Wine'. The EP received a modest response from Irish radio…

On September 25, 2013, Rubyworks posted a free video for 'Take Me to Church' on the Internet music site Bandcamp. The video was made on a very modest budget of around €1,500.

Within two days of posting it on the internet, it attracted the attention of Stephen Fry, the celebrated English actor, television host and gay rights activist. The video featured two guys who were assaulted by gay-bashing vigilantes and a scene with two males kissing. It was a hard-hitting protest against the antagonism towards the gay community practised by the Catholic Church and anti-gay governments such as that of Vladimir Putin in Russia. Hozier himself does not appear in the video.

Fry was inspired to tweet about the video to his 19 million followers, and within another 48 hours, it had achieved 250,000 views increasing by 5/6,000 every hour. It was this remarkable reaction to the video that sparked the avalanche of e-mails I'd received from the global music industry.

If this sort of frenzy happens at all, it usually takes place after an artist has had a chart hit with a record, but the Hozier situation had taken on a life of its own. So, this was going to be no normal week after all, especially when I recalled that Hozier was due to play only his second ever live concert that coming Thursday, October 3, in The Button Factory in Dublin and it was one concert I could not miss.

The growing global interest in Hozier was reinforced by the fact that there were 41 A&R* representatives from music companies all over the world at that sell-out gig, all eager to either sub-publish* the rights for the world for Hozier's recordings and his songs, or even to sign him and his songs directly. This was an extraordinary turn of events. When the Internet took off, the doomsayers had foretold that this sort of music industry frenzy, common in the past, would never happen in the digital era, not least because the Internet was awash with free music and CD sales were in sharp decline.

The Rubyworks record label and Evolving Music Publishing are run by a compact, highly professional and experienced team. Both companies are owned by Denis and Caroline, and now also act as management for Hozier. Niall Muckian runs Rubyworks, with label managers Roger Quail and Eoin Aherne, while I was the administrator for the Evolving Publishing catalogue, we all swung into action in response to the impact of the video. I had already started to respond to the e-mails that were continuing to flood in and confirmed to each one that I was indeed the man to talk to if you wanted to sub-publish Hozier songs for the rest of the world.

I hadn't yet realised this was going to be the most exciting and the most demanding year I'd ever had in a career that was not without its fair share of successes. In fact, I'm not even sure if Hozier himself realised the storm of interest his music was creating. I knew I had to stay calm and act professionally. I'd been in music publishing since 1979 and had a lot of experience to draw on from my various dealings on the international scene. But, on that Monday morning I also instinctively knew that I was facing an enormous challenge with big stakes, and was determined to maximise the benefits for both myself and my clients. I immediately encouraged all interested parties, especially the major international publishers Warner-Chappell, Universal and Sony ATV Publishing, the most powerful music publishing houses in the world, to outline whatever offer they wanted to place before us, so I could examine its implications and, hopefully in time, go with the best one.

One of the first to call me on my mobile phone was James Dewar, the A&R* director of Sony ATV/EMI Music. By coincidence, he was on holidays in Italy but was so enthusiastic about the Hozier song and video he was willing to cut his holiday short in order to meet me in Dublin and attend the gig. I was impressed with his enthusiasm… more anon.

I was happy to meet him, and he asked me, as we'd never met, how he might recognise me-

'Do you drink Guinness, I asked him?' 'Yes' he said, so we agreed to meet in the small bar of the Clarence Hotel in Dublin (owned by a couple of members of U2!) and I told him he should look for a bald, bearded guy with his own drink and a spare pint of Guinness on the table. And that's exactly how it turned out. My instinct warned me this could be a hugely significant meeting, but I also knew how important it was not to get carried away in the excitement. Decades of experience in the music business taught me caution.

I'd seen too many people squander opportunities by either accepting the first offer presented to them or by baulking at really good offers and allowing them to pass, as I'd done myself.

So, I was really performing a balancing act under considerable pressure, aware of the immense responsibility I bore for the rest of the team, including Hozier himself. Whether I kept my nerve or fell off, will be revealed in due course, after I tell you about my background, and how and why I got into the music business in the first place.

I'll also tell you how the amazing Hozier story panned out and recount some of my adventures at work and at play in the unpredictable world of the music industry at home and abroad…

Chapter Two

THE EARLY YEARS

I was born in 1950 to parents of mixed religion who hailed from the town of Portadown in Northern Ireland. My Grandmother on my Dad's side was Protestant, and he had married a Catholic, very unusual in the staunchly-Protestant Portadown of that time. One of my Grandfathers was killed while serving with the British Army in the Great War. My other Grandfather came from the Garvaghy Road, a staunchly republican area. My Mother was Kathleen Beattie, and as a young woman, she'd spent some time in New York in service to a very wealthy Polish-Jewish family. They treated her like their own daughter and she got a tremendous education over there. It also gave her a taste for the high life (not available in Portadown!).

My Father, or 'Pop' as we called him, was John Lappin and he earned his living as a painter/decorator and sign-writer. His first job was actually in the Guild Hall in Belfast. He also became a prominent footballer and was a fine golfer and cricketer. Indeed, they regarded him as something of a 'boy wonder' around Portadown. My sister Joan has described him as 'a tall, beautiful specimen of a man, very handsome'.

He was certainly very presentable and well-spoken; attributes that helped him impress potential business contacts. He was also a very easy-going man who rarely raised his voice and was very fair-minded.

My parents knew each other since their schooldays and had corresponded with each other while Kathleen was in the USA. They got married in Cork, much to the chagrin of our Dad's Mother who told people-

'Our John has run off and married that whore from America.'

My Mother was actually a petite, attractive, dark-haired woman who liked to dress well and once impressed everybody by bringing a bottle of Chanel No 5 perfume back from a trip to Paris.

Kathleen and John were madly in love and I grew up in a very happy home. At that time in Portadown, mixed marriages were actively discouraged, but our family wasn't religious at all. She'd occasionally sing, 'The Old Bog Road' just to annoy some of the relatives! But we'd often go to watch the parade on the 'Twelfth' (of July) and enjoy the genial banter (which later on became very ungenial and tragic) between the marchers and the spectators.

1933 Mum & Dad on the banks of the Bann

The religious and political tensions in Portadown, along with an offer Pop received to play for Bohemians football club in Dublin, encouraged my parents to move south of the border to Dublin in 1939. The move was a smooth one and not a wrench of any kind. My Mother was keen to get away from Pop's Mother as they never got on anyway, although we often went back to Portadown for holidays and to see friends and relations.

SHELBOURNE V DRUMCONDRA JAN. 1934

1934 Dad playing for Shelbourne F.C.

There were four children in our family, Peggy, Des, Joan and myself. Although only Peggy and Des were born in the North and Joan and I in the South, we always considered ourselves to be a Northern family. Thus, internal family issues were dealt with in the Northern way, brought out into the open, discussed vigorously and after a decision was taken we all moved on with no further rancour or animosity. But, even after we moved to Dublin we went up to enjoy the 'Twelfth' merely as a social event, a good day out. We'd see the blood running down the hands of the lambeg drummers, they bashed their drums so vigorously.

I used to play with a boy called Charlie during such visits to my 'hometown', but he wasn't allowed to play with me on 'The Twelfth'. It wasn't until I was about 10 that I discovered the Twelfth of July celebrations commemorated the victory of the Protestant King William of Orange over the Catholic King James at the Battle of The Boyne in 1690. This battle has divided the Catholic and Protestant communities in Northern Ireland ever since.

After the move to Dublin, Dad, who was also a builder, started his painting and decorating business in Dolphin's Barn. The family moved around a lot because he'd build a house, we'd move into it for a time, he'd sell it and then start building another. When I was born we had a very large house, 99 Trees Road in Mount Merrion, a lovely location in suburban Dublin. In fact, all the houses on that road were built by my Dad.

We were a reasonably affluent family, and my Mother encouraged Pop to get on in his business. But, as he became more successful business-wise he also became a bit of a high flyer and was absent from the home more often. He became friends with the Irish boxer and singer Jack Doyle who was a major celebrity in his day. My Mother actually had her photo taken with Jack. Kathleen was in her forties when she became pregnant with me, a situation she found hard to cope with. She took to drinking and lost herself in books, including the classics and modern novels. She was very literary and often made up word-games for us. She wasn't a natural social animal and was self-reliant enough not to really need people.

My sisters Peggy and Joan were drawn to the acting profession, probably picking up on my Mother's artistic leanings. They were sent to dancing school and looked and dressed very alike, although Peggy tended to be a lot cheekier. Mother's interest in songs possibly sparked my own later interest in entertainment. She used to take me on her knee, tell me stories about songs, and sing ballads to me, including 'Boolavogue', a strange fact given that I later moved to Enniscorthy, about 10 miles from the pleasant village that gave its name to the song.

My brother Des was born between the two sisters, so all three of my siblings were in their teens by the time I was born, and my Mother was 42, so I suppose I'd be entitled to regard myself as an afterthought, or as some might remark, a mistake! Des tended to get into trouble as a kid. He'd give back-chat to Pop and was the real rebel of the family.

As kids, we got on very well, despite the age difference, so much so that those positive relationships lasted into adulthood. But even at an early age, I developed a somewhat forceful attitude, so that my older siblings started to refer to me as 'The General'!

When I was about 3 and while my parents were away, Peggy and Joan came up with the bright idea of painting me in soot they got from the chimney. They thought this was great fun, although my parents didn't when they returned and saw the state of me.

1953 Joan, Johnny, Peggy and Des feeding the ducks in St Stephen's Green

One afternoon when I was about 4 and on my way to a school fair, I was challenged by a woman outside our house at 99 Trees Road.

'So what age are you now, little boy?' she demanded to know.

'4', I said defiantly to what to me looked like an *auld one* but who was probably little more than eighteen or twenty.

'And what school do you go to?' she further enquired.

'Sion Hill,' I replied.

My Mother used to say that Dad was 'Penny wise and Pound foolish'. He didn't mind large bills, but he hated giving out small amounts of cash. One day while heading to a school fair, Pop tossed me a shilling (about 5p), following the badgering I'd waged over lunch. But minutes later, on the No. 5 bus to Sion Hill, I began feeling very sorry for myself when I heard the other children comparing what their parents had given them to spend at the fair.

'I've got two shillings and sixpence' (a little more than 12p) ventured one, 'My Mother gave me five shillings' (a whopping 25p), boasted another. It seemed they all had more money than I had. I was very disappointed.

Another abiding memory from my innocent Sion Hill schooldays was the gym mistress. She'd do a 'Drill Routine' based on a fireman going up a ladder. She always wore bright red satin knickers, which were amply displayed for all to see. This garment always fascinated me, but back then I didn't understand why!

It was tough having a brother and sisters so much older than me, but it had its rewards. I remember badgering (I was good at that!) my sister Joan for a ride on her Lambretta scooter when she came home from her work at lunchtime. She took me up and down to the end of the road where the family doctor lived until either time or her patience ran out. She also tells the story of me receiving a toy truck as a Christmas present from my Mother and, much to my Mother's displeasure, kicking it around the house. My Mother said-

'Johnny, you can't kick an inanimate object,' and I replied-

'That's not an inanimate object, that's a bloody old lorry that won't go.'

So the impatience that many of my friends and work colleagues witness today will tell you, it's a trait I never grew out of and was a factor from way back then also.

The one *official* photo I have of Pop, from 1954, shows him proudly wearing the Badge of Office as President of the Master Painters & Decorators Association of Ireland. He regularly attended dinners and a range of other functions, and he always seemed to be either away or preparing to go away to the UK, Canada and elsewhere. Indeed, so frequent were his absences from the home that my Mother dubbed him 'the man who comes to dinner'. As I later discovered, he was also a talent scout for top English football clubs such as Millwall and Charlton Athletic in London. I was often brought along on such business trips to the UK and travelled frequently in the various team coaches. These were impressive adventures for an 8 or 9-year-old, so life seemed pretty good!

We weren't a particularly close or religious family and were all encouraged to develop our own personalities and I was blissfully unaware of a growing rift between my parents. I came home from school several times to find my Mother passed out on the floor from an excess of alcohol. I would happily accept the casual explanations that Mammy isn't well or suchlike excuses, and I suspect her alcoholism may have been precipitated by Dad's regular absences, and having me at such a comparatively late stage in life might have been an added pressure.

*1954 Official photo of Dad as President of the
Master Painters and Decorators.*

During the early 60s we briefly lived in various residences around Dublin, including Walkinstown and Ranelagh, and moved into 22 Rathmore Avenue, Kilmacud in the early sixties. That constant moving around could've been the source of my life-long tendency towards impatience, because no sooner would we get settled in one place where I'd make friends, when we were preparing to move on and I'd have to start all over again somewhere else.

But, the Rathmore Avenue house played a significant role in my future, and it was while living there that I made long-standing friendships with Ken Grace, Willy Redmond and Charlie McNally all of whom I still remain friends with, over fifty years later! In those days you could walk from the Upper Kilmacud Road to the Three Rock Mountains through fields that are now occupied by the Sandyford Industrial Estate. We had many happy summer days exploring the *Res* (Leopardstown Reservoir) and trying to entice the local young ladies to come for a walk, while furtively wishing for pursuits of a far more horizontal kind.

Pop had a motor mower for cutting grass, quite a wonder in the early sixties, and Ken Grace and I used it to start our first entrepreneurial venture,

Johnny & Ken's Motor Mowing Service, the object of which was to extract two shillings from the local residents in return for cutting their grass with this wonderful new invention. The enterprise was short-lived, however, as the principals couldn't agree whose name should come first in the aforementioned business name! True to form my Dad was also looking for a 'cut' of the profits.

Immediately following the FA Cup final in May 1964, I was playing football in the back field and dreaming I was my football hero Stanley Matthews when Pop called me into the house. My Mother had quietly passed away in her sleep at the age of 52. I was only 14 at the time, a vulnerable age to lose a parent, even though I was probably too young to fully understand it.

In the sad and confused months that followed, I discovered the healing qualities of music. The Beatles were taking the world (and me) by storm, and I threw myself headlong into this wonderful new revolution. My sisters having married and moved out, I discovered Pop wasn't a great cook, so we lived on a diet of burgers and chips. That might help explain why I never became much of a foodie and I'm still quite unadventurous when eating out.

My Dad married his second wife Bridie in August 1964. She was a toffee-faced old tart (my exact feelings at the time) and a spinster. She'd worked in the British Embassy in Dublin and had a very plummy, upper-class 1940s British accent. We never got on, in fact, it was more like hate-at-first-sight. She totally resented me because I was still living at home, so I spent a lot of time living elsewhere instead.

For nearly five years I lived happily in the Dublin suburb of Dundrum with my sister Joan and her husband Liam, as well as their offspring, the singer Leslie Dowdall and film and documentary maker Barrie Dowdall, and their siblings Siobhan and Gavin. I stayed with them from Christmas 1964 until 1968, and the stability and welcome they afforded me during this time contrasted completely with my earlier disrupted family life. For the first time ever I lived in a normal family situation. I also spent time with a close friend Willy Redmond whose parents were from Carlow and they'd take me there on weekends. They were very generous, despite there being no family ties. There too I saw the value of a close and loving family that was all new to me.

Given the nature of Dad's work, we'd lived a very nomadic life, so my education was quite fragmented. From Sion Hill in Blackrock, I made my Holy Communion in Rathmines where I then went to school. And after we settled in Rathmore Avenue in Stillorgan I attended the Christian Brothers Oatlands College nearby. Looking back now, my schooling is a blur, because of all the changes, but there's one unpleasant incident that stuck with me. I was in the Oatlands schoolyard one day playing soccer when one of the Christian Brother teachers challenged me, asking me why I was playing a foreign game.

I replied, 'What are you talking about, foreign game?' For this, he delivered a kick to my stomach. Pop was a very good soccer player who'd played in the League of Ireland for Shelbourne and Bohemians, and for Portadown in the Irish League before he became a talent scout. When I told him what the Brother did to me for playing soccer he was outraged and went down to the school. I don't know the nature of that discussion, but the upshot of it was I was moved to Blackrock College.

Today, that Brother would almost certainly be charged with assault, but back then Priests and Brothers were a law unto themselves. My experience at Blackrock College was hugely positive and completely different from Oatlands. In Blackrock, often considered as the equivalent of an English public school, you were treated as an individual, whereas in Oatlands you were treated as an anonymous part of a herd. So, it's no surprise it produced so many graduates who became successful in a variety of spheres, including Bob Geldof, rugby international Brian O'Driscoll and indeed, the President of Ireland, Eamon de Valera.

I did my Leaving Certificate (the equivalent of A Levels in the UK) exam at Blackrock when I was 17, getting three honours grades, but I had no particular interest in going to third level education. Even so, Dad persuaded me to undertake a part-time course in Bolton Street College of Technology to study the building trade. I hated it, but I stuck at it and became a qualified, 'Technician of the Institute of Builders', not a qualification that's been of any use to me in my subsequent career!

However, I did pick up two Latin phrases in Bolton Street that I still recall: MERULIUS LACRYMANS and CONIOPHORA CEREBELLA. They mean wet rot and dry rot respectively. So if there's a band out there still looking for a catchy name…

I'd also moved out of Joan and Liam's house and, since moving back in with my Dad and Bridie wasn't an option, I moved into a bedsit near the Country Club in Churchtown. This gave me a sense of independence and I started my first real job working with D&J Lappin Limited, Pops successful painting and decorating business.

He was the J and my brother Des was the D, and at one stage the company employed seventy painters to handle work in Dublin, Meath and Sligo.

We had what we called, 'The Yard', a large building at 7a The Crescent in Monkstown. That's where we kept all the ladders, paint, brushes and other accoutrements of the painting and decorating trade. Pop also had his office there. He insisted I serve my time (become qualified) as a painter so as I would always have a trade. My job was to drive the company van and deliver ladders, paint and painters to the various sites.

I'd pick them up from the yard in Monkstown at 8.30am and set off to the various locations. So, I did learn something that was useful in later life, and that is, whenever I employed a painter to carry out work for me in my various residences, I could tell more or less straight away, by the way he held a brush, if he knew what he was at, or was just another *chancer,* or *Bengal Lancer* as they were called in the trade.

And there was a lot more to learn along the way.

Chapter Three

PAINTING AND DECORATING VERSUS THE MUSIC INDUSTRY

Since the days when I was a small kid, (mind you, I'm still not too tall and I'm perfectly happy to call myself a 'short arse') I'd always felt the pull towards the entertainment industry. It seemed to be so exciting and colourful, and I'd always loved music anyway. My sisters Joan and Peggy, especially the former, had successfully worked as actresses, so that may also have been a factor, although I was too young to see either of them on stage. All three of us may have inherited a sort of artistic bent, possibly from our Mother. Either way, that attraction was there almost from the beginning. At some point, I attended the Brendan Smith Academy for would-be actors in Dublin and remember taking a phone call at home one day. It was the Academy offering me a part in a play in Dublin, but unfortunately, my Mother was having one of her bad spells and I didn't have the bus fare to make the journey. That really disappointed me, but there was nothing I could do about it.

I put on my first ever show when I was 10 years of age. The venue was our garage in our house in Rathmore Avenue, Dublin where I set out benches on concrete blocks for the 'comfort' of the audience and even charged an admission fee. It's interesting that I can't now remember the contents of the show, but I can remember it involved a financial arrangement! The following year I joined the Boy Scouts and sang and danced in their shows, and during my school years, I regularly performed in Gilbert and Sullivan operettas. In fact, I'd been so eager to qualify as a fully-fledged scout I decided to do the required Rawley Test all in one week, much to the amazement of the other boys, as the series of tests usually takes a few months! Predictably, I wanted to qualify immediately for my badge that came with passing these tests.

Of course, it's a substantial leap from merely enjoying performing to wanting to make a full-time career in the music business, as I keep reminding enthusiastic young artists' today.

When I started buying records I picked up albums by The Clancy Brothers, The Beatles and the American folkie Tom Paxton. The radio was nearly always playing in the house and I even made a vain attempt to play the guitar. I tried to copy Paxton's finger-picking style but didn't have the patience to learn it fully. I started my, *ahem*, performing career as a singer and drummer in 1964 at the age of 14, although I pretended I was 16. The usual tendency, especially regarding female performers, has been the reverse, to pretend to be younger.

The dominant live musical entertainment in Ireland at the time was provided by the showbands, who used to traverse the country but they mainly performed covers of pop hits and standards, and that didn't appeal to a young rebel like me. I wanted to do something more creative, like other bands of that era such as Granny's Intentions, Orange Machine, Horselips and Sleepy Hollow (who, incidentally, were managed by a lad called Denis Desmond!). While playing on the local rock circuit I really caught the bug, but it also became apparent to me that I wasn't much of a singer, although some might argue that such a drawback hasn't always been an impediment to success! I wasn't a brilliant drummer either!

But,' Fuck it,' I thought, I was determined to make a life in music.

One of my first bands was called Five Against Fate, I was on co-lead vocals and the line-up included drummer Paddy Feeney who later established himself as a major player in Dublin's sound hire business. Five Against Fate had business cards printed offering our services for Parties, Dances and Funerals… PDF! I may have actually been the first to come up with that, although I forgot to copyright it! (LOL!)

We played around the community and parish halls in the Mount Merrion area. One of the highlights of our short-lived career was supporting Them, (who'd enjoyed several UK chart hits) in Stella House in Mount Merrion. Their lead singer was Van Morrison, and I was mightily impressed by their songs and strong stage performance. We learned to play one of their hits, 'Gloria' and it featured in our set from then on. But, as is the nature of young bands, we eventually split.

Yet, I still harbored a sense of determination that I applied to just about everything that seemed important to me. For example, when I was 16 I seriously wanted my own motorbike. But when I told my Dad about my plan he looked at me and said-

'That's very interesting, Johnny. How are you going to afford it?'

So, Ken Grace, whom I'd known since I was about 5, and I went over to London where we got ourselves summer jobs working for Lyons Maid in Hammersmith who produced a brand of cakes, ice-creams and ice-lollies. I pretended to be 18 and took on the most boring jobs imaginable. One consisted of a conveyor belt job where Swiss Rolls came along and my job was to take them two at a time, roll them in sugar, and transfer them to another conveyor belt.

Another job was packing boxes with bottles of squash. There would be three of us who'd pack four bottles each in the conveyor of boxes coming down the line. To amuse ourselves, as we got more proficient at the different tasks, we'd hold up the conveyor belt so a new recruit further down the line would have none coming to him for a while, and then, as we released those we were holding back, a deluge of them would arrive together, sending him into a tizzy.

I did menial work like that for 8 tedious hours every day, although the money was good and I was getting closer to that coveted motorbike. In time I got my bike, but I also recall one serious, life-defining moment.

I was sitting by the River Thames one sunny summer's day on a lunch break from Lyons Maid and reflecting on the repetitive nature of life as a factory worker. I resolved there and then that it was definitely not the life for me.

When I got back to Dublin, I ventured onto the cabaret scene with my friend John O'Sullivan in a duo we called Ad-Lib. We wore frilly (loud) orange shirts, with gold braided black bolero waistcoats. We performed twenty-minute sets in the booming cabaret lounges around Dublin, often playing three venues in one night. When we were taken on by a 'manager' who booked these gigs, we thought we were on our way to worldwide fame and fortune! The fact that I couldn't really sing didn't bother me! We did no original songs, but it was great fun. During one of our performances in the Drake Inn, in Finglas on the Northside of Dublin, we were in the middle of 'The Fool On The Hill' by The Beatles when a drunk in the front row came up and loudly demanded we play 'La Bamba', the Latino pop hit. He made me realise that I didn't really want to be a singing jukebox for drunks like the fool in the front row, so I soon decided to explore other options in the business.

I still had the full-time job with my Dad's company, which in truth, I really hated. I wasn't overly enamored with having to arrive at building sites at 8.30am on freezing mornings to boil water for the tea in a billy-can, but this was part of Pop's insistence that I serve my time as a painter. I suppose the uncertainty and high risk pertaining to any career in the music business turns it into a negative for many people, including Pop, as you can be in the charts one week and in the dole queue the next.

Pensions are a rarity, and it also, unfairly, tends to be seen as an easy job that attracts lazy people- 'money for nothing and your chicks for free' as Mark Knopfler once sarcastically sang. In reality, people have little idea as to the hard graft that goes on behind the scenes even with the most musically challenged acts. Undoubtedly, the later successes of Thin Lizzy, U2, The Boomtown Rats, The Cranberries, Sinead O'Connor, The Script, Hozier et al have helped open people's eyes to the commercial potential of a music career, so the disdain Pop felt would probably be less common among parents today.

My girlfriend at that time was Catherine Ellard, a quietly spoken girl who worked as a librarian at UCD in Belfield. She fell pregnant in 1971, when single motherhood was complete taboo, so we got married. Ad-Lib played at our wedding in the Cliff Castle Hotel (now an apartment block) in the coastal suburb of Dalkey on the southside of Dublin, and that was my final public performance as a musician/singer.

Our first baby, Suzanne, was born in January 1972, and we took out a mortgage on our first house in The Donahies in Raheny. I accepted my responsibilities and knew I had to earn money by whatever means I could. I was feeling that my overall situation wasn't very satisfactory or terribly satisfying either, but back then marriages didn't split as easily as they do now. Divorce didn't come to Ireland until 1996, so I knuckled down with my work in the painting and decorating business. The company van came in very handy too when I started doing night-time music gigs, but I was in serious trouble if I was late in the mornings, no matter what the reason was.

One of the painters Pop employed was Dominic Behan, brother of the more famous writer Brendan, who was also a painter. Pop didn't approve of sandpapering, based on the logic that when a painter was sandpapering he wasn't painting and therefore not earning him money. One day he challenged Dominic about this, to which Dominic replied-

'Ah, I think I understand what you're looking for, Mr. Lappin. You want a Michelangelo job in McInerney time'. McInerney's were one of the top Irish building companies at that time.

I was reminded of this story recently when reading Jackie Hayden's book *Love and Theft? Bob Dylan's Celtic Odyssey*. In the sixties, Dominic raised a huge rumpus by claiming that Dylan had copied his 'With God On Our Side' from him. But, when Jackie interviewed Liam Clancy for *Hot Press*, he told him that the air of both songs was actually a traditional tune and that Dominic's claim was nonsense. That story caught my eye, not only because of Behan having been in the family's employ, but also because of my later work revolving around song copyrights.

My brother Des was the apple of Pop's eye. Having been educated at Terenure College he was a very well-read man and was also an excellent carpenter for the family firm. At one point he and I hatched the idea of using 'The Yard' as the base for a retail paint shop, an idea that had the further advantage that my father would be able to access paint at wholesale prices. We called the shop Home and Garden Ltd, and it attracted the attention of a friend Eddie Hanly who was very interested in retail. He suggested we could also sell timber, chipboard and glass cut to the exact size the customer wanted, a service not available at that time anywhere in Dublin.

If you wanted a sheet of glass or timber you had to buy it in the sizes in which the shops bought it, take it home and cut it to size yourself. Des used his carpentry expertise to fit us out with the best saws and other cutting materials, and we even did well selling the off-cuts. I devised a pricing system for 'timber & glass cut to size' and the shop took off immediately. So, over time the Home and Garden business thrived to the point where we had three outlets in Dublin selling all the hardware materials you might need to work in the house or garden.

Better still, its success also enabled me to buy my first new car in 1971, a chocolate brown Ford Capri. I felt I'd really 'arrived' when I was cruising around the city of Dublin in this flash motor.

In the meantime, because of his dependency on alcohol, possibly inherited from my Mother, Des had become somewhat unreliable. That said, he and I got on very well, and we had some great laughs together when he was sober. When Dad took his two foreign holidays every year he'd leave me in charge of the business during these absences. This was a sensible move, as Des with alcohol on board would do daft things. For example, Dad bought him a car which he sold to buy drink, and if there was copper bought in to use on a job, Des would sell it and again use the money for drink. But, me being about 14 years younger than him, Pop's preference for leaving me in charge obviously rankled with Des, so in 1973, during one of Pop's Spanish holidays, Des decided to follow him to Spain to sort this situation out. He'd been drinking heavily prior to my dropping him to the Dun Laoghaire-Holyhead ferry, and before he boarded the ship he looked at me and said-

'You'll do well, Johnny. You're a smart guy.'

As it turned out, these were the last words he ever spoke to me, because he never actually made it to Spain. Two days later I got a phone call from Anne, his wife, telling me Des was dead. He'd been run over by an articulated lorry outside Paris. The driver claimed he'd run out in front of his lorry from a wooded area, but we never really got to the bottom of what happened. I was badly shaken by this tragedy as I loved Des and I knew I'd miss him.

Pop was completely distraught at the tragic news. Indeed, Des was so badly smashed up that his body arrived home in a lead-lined coffin which we were advised not to open. Pop never got over this loss, and he himself died two years later in 1975 of a heart attack, and I reckon, of a broken heart brought on by Des's death. He was 63, and I was 25 years old.

Although, I'd lost both parents and my only brother, Pop left me 4/5ths of the business, a car and a large tax bill!

As I told people at the time, I got 4/5ths of a large headache and a 10-year-old Mini! I also discovered he'd signed ownership of the family home and possessions over to his new wife, Bridie, who was never going to win any popularity contest with my family, and who passed away one year after Pop. She, in turn, left the house and possessions to her relatives, none of whom were known to us Lappins.

One of the bitterest memories I have, and I will take this to my grave, is of the day Joan and I attended the auction of the possessions from our family home. We ourselves had to bid for whatever items we wanted, things we believed should've been ours. If there is an afterlife, Pop will have a lot to answer for. But they say, and occasionally they're right, every cloud has a silver lining, and now, with both my Dad and Des gone, I sold the family painting business to David Dennis, who'd been the company foreman, and closed the door on that forever.

In the meantime, I was also able to close the door on the Home and Garden business which Eddie Hanly and I owned, with my Dad as the silent partner. Eddie was very ambitious and after the success of the outlet in 'The Yard', we had opened a smaller branch in Terenure. While Dad's company was handling the painting of the Northside Shopping Centre we spotted an opening there for a third store. The first weekend of business saw the Northside store jammed with customers.

It appeared to be a considerable success until I checked the stock and realised an enormous level of pilfering had occurred. This was not what I'd planned! The stock had left the shop alright…

My first lesson in the retail world!

One day a woman came into our shop in Monkstown and gave me a detailed list of all the things she wanted in order to build a wardrobe, including locks, screws and pieces of wood of various sizes. I think this brought the final realisation that this (shite) work was in no way as fulfilling as the bits and pieces I'd been doing in music. This was another *lightbulb* moment and I knew the DIY business was not for me. There was a further factor in that the rent on 'The Yard' was about to be increased substantially and it seemed to me it was time to move on. Eddie soldiered on for a short while after until he too decided to call it a day.

Meanwhile, I still loved music and took any little jobs I could fit in around the day job. Instinctively, I knew I needed experience in every aspect of music. I did some roadie* work with John Munnis (now managing Paul Brady) who had a sound hire company in Dublin supplying equipment to acts like Barry Moore, later known as Luka Bloom. I put up posters, worked as a sound engineer, was a lighting technician for various bands and was basically happy to do any job that would give me a practical insight into how the music business worked.

I also wanted to do things I enjoyed, and while I've always liked making money, I've never wanted it to be the over-riding factor in what I worked at. I considered it essential to have a working knowledge of every aspect of the music business, a belief I still hold today for anyone considering a career in the music business. I went to many gigs and concerts, and one of those gigs made a major impression on me. It was in Toners on Baggot Street, Dublin, and the band was Fag Ash Lil, featuring a young guy who looked about 12. His name, I later discovered, was Paul Brady and he went on to become one of Ireland's most revered songwriters and performers. Fag Ash Lil later morphed into Stepaside, and I became a big fan of their good-time rock'n'roll sound and their exciting live gigs. I went as often as I could to their Dublin gigs, including regular Sunday afternoon shows at the Merrion Inn, known locally as the M1, which they used to pack out.

After a while, I became quite friendly with the band members. I'd noticed they couldn't get any more people into their Merrion Inn gigs, and in conversation asked them where they thought they could progress to next. They had little answer to that, other than-

1975 Steapaside

'We need to get out of here, that's for sure.'

So, I was probably about 25 when the germ of an exciting idea took root. Why don't I merge the business experience I'd gained from working in Pop's company with my love for music? And I devised this cunning plan. The aforementioned Stella House, where as a teenager I'd go to dances on a Saturday night, and where I'd become so besotted by Them, was now a pub called The Sportsman's Inn. It was a sizeable space with lots of potential, and furthermore, I knew Dave Whitren, the owner. So, I called around to his house, and when he answered the door I cheekily asked him-

'How would you like to take in £1,000 in your bar between 4pm and 7pm on Sunday afternoons?'

'Come in, young man,' he said.

I outlined my plan but I didn't tell him the band I had in mind was Stepaside. In fact, I hadn't informed them of my plan either!

So, having gotten Mr Whitren's enthusiastic response, I explained to the band what I had in mind, *only* if they let me manage them.

Initially, they were sceptical, not least because I was younger than them, but when I explained they could double their audience and their income, they paid serious attention. So, that's how I began my career in the music business, getting my foot in the door as Stepaside's manager.

I was amused years later to discover that one of the first successful record companies in the USA, National Records, was set up by a guy called Al Green who'd also come from the painting business and who had a massive number 1 hit with 'Kansas City' by Wilbert Harrison.

In spite of my age and inexperience of the music scene, I was very confident I could make this work. I knew I was a reliable organiser, as proven by my work in Pop's company, where my duties included keeping the accounts, and doing the wages using a ready reckoner (ask one of your grandparents!). I was persistent and determined and felt I had the ability to deal with people and the instinct to suss out the time-wasters from those who could *actually* do something.

Although, later the role of manager embraced such responsibilities as negotiating, recording and publishing contracts, back then the primary role of a manager was to get gigs, and it's ironic to see in the modern digital age, live performance is again the main income stream for most acts around the globe. Latterly, the role of the manager has sometimes been likened to combining that of babysitter and nanny, taking care of the immature whims of precocious and self-obsessed pop and rock stars, but there was none of that with Stepaside. They were mature individuals and experienced musicians who wanted to enjoy playing and make some money… Simple! They were rightly sceptical of my managerial ability, but when I convinced them they could draw 600 or 700 of the beautiful people to the Sportsman's on Sunday afternoons, their confidence in me grew. Quickly, it became the gig the hipsters had to be seen at, and our partnership blossomed.

Around that time I also spotted there were no rock'n'roll gigs in the heavily populated and affluent Dun Laoghaire area. So, I scoured the town in search of a suitable venue and found one called Rosses Hotel (now an apartment block) that was recently built and run by two ambitious young brothers from Longford. I proposed putting on a late-night rock gig every Monday featuring three bands, including Stepaside, The Jimi Slevin Band and a special appearance by an up-and-coming local band of the day.

Another close friend, Charlie McNally, was as keen to be part of the music scene as I was, and one of our first projects was to run gigs which we titled 'Rock On At Rosses' and even had t-shirts designed and printed with that slogan. But it was necessary back then to provide food in order to get a late-night bar license, which we duly acquired. So, for the opening night, we were expecting an audience of 200/250 people who had to be fed. I was living with my wife Cathy in Watsons, near Killiney at the time, and the two of us plus Charlie and his wife Margo decided to provide our own version of Chicken Fricassee.

Unfortunately, we didn't have a pot big enough for the demanding task in hand, so we decided to use our bath, paying little attention to the health and safety issues of the time, although the bath was new and spotlessly clean. With the food cooked, we transported it to the venue in large black sacks and doled out helpings onto paper plates. When we opened the doors the fans flooded in, in the anticipated numbers. I took the money at the door, handed over the food tickets, and passed them on to Charlie who in turn took the food tickets and referred them over to our two wives who were dishing out the food. But, unknown to me, the customers, having given Charlie their tickets, on reaching the food tables could ask for any number of plates and the wives had no way of knowing if this was ok. Back at the door, I was assuming all was going swimmingly until Charlie came over and told me we were out of food.

I said- 'Charlie, we can't be out of food. We made enough for at least 250 people and we've only let 175 in so far.'

We were in a state of mild panic wondering what to do when a drunk came up to me with a plate of food, and sneeringly said-

'What's this shite, Kit-e-Kat?' referring to a popular brand of tinned cat food. I said- 'At 19p a tin? You must be fuckin' joking!'

Anyway, we had little option but to spread the remaining food around on other plates and we were more careful about handing it out this time. The night worked out fine in the end, and it was the first of a successful series of gigs that ran until local residents objected to the noise level and we were forced to stop. In one sense this was a manifestation of the antagonism society in general had towards rock music which, to their narrow minds, was peopled by long-haired louts who drank, smoked and made an infernal racket that in no way could be called music.

Determined to press on with my new-found career as a manager, I went into Eason's on O'Connell Street and bought a copy of every provincial newspaper they stocked. Going meticulously through each one, I spent weeks making a crude database of every entertainment venue in the country, compiling a rather primitive forerunner of the *Hot Press Yearbook* that came about a few years later. Obviously, there was no internet in those days and I can now smile at how quickly this could be done online these days.

In 1976, I set up a promotions company specifically to handle my activities and called it JTF Promotions, after the recently released Thin Lizzy album *Johnny The Fox*. But, I was still naive in many respects and had much to learn. I hadn't realised how highly competitive and somewhat cut-throat the music industry was. I learned very quickly though, mainly because I had to.

In later years the Irish music industry developed a community aspect that involved a fair amount of socialising through which you could meet other people in the business, form alliances and exchange ideas. But, there was little of that back in the mid-seventies, and you had to fly solo and learn through your own efforts as well as your mistakes.

The music scene was heavily dominated by the lucrative showbands, known as 'cover' bands* today and it wasn't uncommon for their managers to book their bands for an entire year ahead and take out advertisements boasting that their diary for the coming year was full. But I didn't care much for the showband management approach which would have a band playing Killarney one night, Letterkenny the next, and Cork the next, as if the venues were picked by throwing darts at a dartboard. I had more 'artistic' aspirations and felt I could organise things better than that.

There was little co-operation or interaction between the showband scene and the rock band scene. In fact, they were poles apart on most matters and fairly antagonistic towards each other at times. It was virtually impossible for rock bands to get bookings in ballrooms until the showband managers started using them as cheap 'relief' bands to kick start the night and provide a sharp contrast to the main act. The rock band's casual appearance, long hair and general lack of conformity, plus the fact that they rarely played many hit tracks, set the audience up to welcome the main act with open arms, and considerable relief. Then the top act came on in their matching shiny suits, tidy haircuts and repertoire of well-known tunes, in most cases copied note for note from the records. If only out of politeness, someone from the showband would call for a show of appreciation for the support band but were often greeted with either a desultory handclap or two or even complete silence and indifference.

Showbands also dominated our one and only national radio station, Radio Eireann (now known as RTE Radio 1). Much of the station's output consisted of sponsored 15-minute programmes, most of which were recorded in Eamon Andrews Studios in Harcourt Street and controlled by the showband 'mafia'. It was generally rumoured in the business, although no convincing evidence was ever produced, that payola* was rife.

So there was little airtime for Irish rock music, but lots of it for Irish showbands, ballad groups and middle-of-the-road acts. It was also commonly accepted that several showband managers bought hundreds, if not thousands, of records by their own bands in order to skew the charts because a hit single not only upped the profile of the band but could also be used as a bargaining tool for higher fees for live appearances. It's said the Bog of Allen is full of those records waiting to be discovered by archaeologists of the future who will no doubt scratch their heads in wonderment over these strange plastic artefacts from a bygone age.

Undoubtedly, the showbands were more geared towards giving the punters what they wanted. They also provided the social occasions, in many areas the only ones, where young men and women could meet, although, in true *Ballroom of Romance* style, their usual starting positions were at opposite sides of the ballroom. Many dances were run by and supervised by local parish priests. No alcohol could be sold, but there was plenty of tea, crisps and minerals, as soft drinks were called back in those days.

Whereas many Irish newspapers today cover the popular music scene on an almost daily basis, back in the seventies coverage was restricted to maybe a column or two at the weekends. So there was scant opportunity for rock bands to build a profile when most of the available space was dedicated to the more commercial end of the business. But, that didn't deter us. In fact, the challenges might even have spurred us on. So in August 1977, Stepaside released their first single, a version of the R'n'B standard 'Good Mornin' Little Schoolgirl', on the independent Mulligan label. It probably wouldn't be acceptable in today's PC world, but we launched it with a reception in the Sportsman's Inn and encouraged everyone to come dressed as schoolgirls and schoolboys which most of the punters did and this (naughty) event just added to the weekly crowd attending the gig.

It became a good time rock n' roll show for the 'beautiful' people of the day. I thought I was well on my way to fame and fortune (again!).

I further branched out to run weekend gigs in the Mississippi Rooms in Bray, north Co Wicklow. But the cut-throat nature of the business finally caught up with me that same month when Stepaside were booked to play at one of Ireland's first ever major outdoor festivals at Dalymount Park, with Thin Lizzy headlining while the rest of the bill included The Boomtown Rats, Fairport Convention, Stagalee and The Radiators From Space.

In the build-up to the event, I was telling the production manager we needed access to bring in our drum kit and other backline equipment when he quietly told me all that stuff would be provided. I argued that my band preferred to use their own equipment. A discussion ensued which ended with me saying-

'So, what you're saying is, if we don't use the equipment provided by you, we won't be on the bill?' And he said,-'Exactly!' That was another valuable lesson learned.

The gig was a huge success, not least for The Boomtown Rats and their effusive frontman Bob Geldof, but that experience made me even more determined to find my own niche in which to carve out a full-time long-term career in the music business. I knew that band management meant dealing with egos, some even as big as Geldof's, and the usual bickering, petty jealousies and in-fighting you get because one person thinks he or she is not getting enough attention or money or praise.

The Dalymount experience showed me the level of grief that went hand-in-hand with being a concert promoter at the top level, and I began to realise

I wasn't attracted down that career path either.

I began to look to the broader industry to see where my future might lie. On my way to the Macroom Festival in Cork, a major highlight of the rock music calendar, one of the guys travelling in the car with me said he knew a lot about the music business but wished he knew more about music publishing. The only publishing I was really familiar with was the publishing of books, newspapers and magazines, but music publishing was a different business altogether. I knew little or nothing about it, so I set out to find out more.

I quickly discovered that the laws of most western countries recognise the concept of copyright, and music publishing deals with the copyright in songs and compositions. It means, in theory at least, nobody can legally use a piece of music, whether on a record, in concert, in a film, TV commercials or on the radio, or in any public place, without paying the company or person who legally owns the copyright of that work.

On making further enquiries, I found that few people in Ireland seemed to know very much about the subject, and fewer still worked at it. I could see the advantages right from the start, and began to see the job as one of managing songs, and reflected that songs wouldn't argue with me, or turn up late for meetings, or get drunk before going on stage, or piss me off like bands pissed off their managers all over the world or upset key figures in their own careers or get lost in nightclubs. They didn't phone you in the middle of the night expecting you to sort out their marital difficulties or find a mechanic to fix their car. No, songs were relatively trouble-free, and music publishing had an order about it that appealed to my naturally tidy mind.

So in short, I spotted a job opportunity, went for it full tilt and, several decades later, am still at it. And I owe it all to a casual remark from a man in the back seat of a car somewhere between Dublin and Macroom in 1978. I know that man to this day but won't name him to protect his innocence… Hi, Billy!

And what a long, strange trip that turned out to be!

Chapter Four

THE SCOFF YEARS

In the early 1970s, one of the centres of the showband business was in the Westland building in Lombard Street, Dublin. The complex included Lombard Recordings Studios, as well as the offices of top showband managers like Brian Molloy (Cotton Mill Boys), Tom Costello (Johnny McEvoy), George O'Reilly (Dermot O'Brien), Michael O'Riordan (road-managed The Dixies), Mick Clerkin (Larry Cunningham), Donie Cassidy (Foster and Allen), Tom Doherty (The Miami) and Jim Hand (Furey Brothers). It was like the Brill Building* of the Irish music industry, and despite coming from the rock'n'roll wing of the business, I was determined to get both feet in the door. And I saw Lombard Street as a possible way in.

I became friendly with Michael O'Riordan who'd started in music publishing but was way ahead of me at the time. I persuaded him I was a young buck with something to offer, so he took me on to work with him. His first step was to give me a ledger he used, to keep track of music publishing payments, for songwriters he'd signed. That money generally came in from the PRS (Performing Rights Society) and the MCPS (Mechanical Copyright Protection Society). This work had to be carried out by hand, as there were no computers back then, and I was given a handwritten list of percentages that had been agreed with the writers to be paid out on each song. The work required close attention to detail, luckily a skill I'd learned in Pop's business.

I'd already had some dealings with Jim Hand who managed a variety of

Irish acts, including the ballad singer Paddy Reilly, who would later have a huge hit with 'The Fields of Athenry'. The Furey Brothers who made 'The Green Fields of France' an international hit and comedian Brendan Grace, and who saw that this rock business, which he'd previously despised, might have some money in it. He had a high profile and he told Stepaside, more or less, never mind this young Lappin bloke, I'm a real manager. So they fired me! I was so naive I didn't know I should've had them sign a contract with me. Another lesson.

1989 Music Industry Golf Society with Joe Dolan,
Jim Hand and Brian Molloy.

I later heard Jim boasting to his cronies, that very same morning; he'd received a cheque for £20,000 from RCA Records in London who were avid to sign Stepaside. I don't believe the band ever released anything for RCA, but it was typical of the bullshit one-upmanship Jim and his ilk indulged in.

I'd been approached by a band called The Time Machine who'd only recently parted company with their own manager Louis Walsh, yes, the same Louis who later made a name for himself as a judge on *The X-Factor* television talent show and as manager of Boyzone, Westlife, Jedward and numerous other acts.

The Time Machine line-up included David Jameson from a well-known family of jewelers. As if to prove I could do a neat line in bullshit myself, I told them they couldn't afford to take me on as a manager, as they'd need a PA system, a van to get them to gigs, keyboards and so on. But the Jameson guy had access to money, so a few weeks later they came back and told me they had all these essentials.

I capitulated, for a short while, and then became their manager. One of the venues I booked them into was Archbolds in Carlow run by a guy called Robert Archbold. Robert told me he was thinking of bringing in a top English act, the hit-making act David Essex, to the venue. He asked if I thought this artist would 'take the door' (a music industry euphemism for accepting the money paid in on the night rather than commit to an actual fee).

I thought this was hilarious, and replied-

'Would he take the door? He'd take the door, the roof and the fuckin' hinges.'

He clearly had no idea how top level international acts operated. But that lack of awareness would've been prevalent in the showband world, and among the showband heads.

Stepaside, having (predictably) broken up, I started working with the band's singer Deke O'Brien, and we set up an independent rock record company Scoff Records, which we based in the Lombard St building. Deke was in quite a few bands previously, such as Bluesville (who had a top ten USA hit with a single called 'You Turn Me On'), The Action and Nightbus, and he convinced me the time was right to start up an Indie Irish rock label. Deke and I wore satin jackets, had long hair and loved loud music, so the Lombard Street people looked at us as if we were aliens from the Planet Zog. They repeatedly told us there was no money in rock'n'roll (although it wouldn't be long before U2 proved otherwise, and they'd presumably never heard of Elvis Presley or The Beatles?).

The Show banders, as we called them used to mockingly call me 'Street Level'. Donie Cassidy, a manager and later a senator, said to me one day during a chat in the local Lombard St pub-

'Look, Street Level, you're a man with a lot of energy but there's no money in that rock'n'roll stuff. Why don't you get an act that'll actually sell, like

Foster and Allen, and make some real money?' He was managing them at the time, but I was having none of it. I said-

'Look, Donie, if you're going up to the bar to buy a round would you make mine a luger and lime.' A luger being a type of German handgun and I'd rather have used one on myself than get involved in that sort of leprechaun PaddyWhackery music.

In return for doing the ledger work for Michael O 'Riordan's publishing companies, Deke and I were given an office in the building which measured 9 feet x 6 feet to run the record label from. As a bit of a diversion, we hired a very attractive girl who was an ex-heroin addict and whom I nicknamed 'the Staff'. In order to irritate the other guys in the building, we'd bang the wall as if there was some kind of sexual activity going on. This sparked widespread rumours as to what Lappin and O'Brien were up to with 'the Staff'. Some evenings in the local pub she'd sit on our knees in a very short mini skirt to help fuel these rumours. Despite the fact there was nothing remotely untoward happening, their reaction used to crack us up.

In essence, Scoff Records was Ireland's first dedicated rock music label. We released records by such notable Irish rock acts like The Atrix, The Rhythm Kings, The Outfit, Koklin, Mama's Boys and Stano. Being part of the Lombard Street operation meant I had access to downtime in the in-house recording studio run by Deirdre Costello who looked sympathetically on what we were trying to do, so we could make recordings at minimal cost.

We didn't have a defined policy as to what acts to sign, but we enthusiastically avoided anything that might smack of showbands, ballad groups or middle-of-the-road music. We instinctively sought out interesting rock musicians who could play well, were out there gigging and were hungry for success. As virtually the only serious outlet for rock acts looking for an indie label to record for, we were probably their first port of call, so we didn't exactly have to scour the country.

At that time Deke, from his past experiences, knew a little more than I did about publishing, so I grandiosely suggested we should have a *publishing division* and form a publishing company. He said, 'You're a real dark horse, aren't you?' And I said, 'No I'm a dark fox!' a throw-back to the name of my promotions company Johnny The Fox. And so we called our publishing company Dark Fox Music and set it up as an arm of Scoff, and all Scoff songs were published by Dark Fox. My music publishing career was off and running…

*

In 1976, Cathy had our second child Jonathan, so in order to make some real money, I joined forces with a guy called Joe McMahon, and we started to run the entertainment for the summer season in a now-defunct hotel in Curracloe, Co Wexford. I'd worked with Joe when he and Eddie Hanly ran a Kentucky Fried Chicken-type outlet in Kilmainham in Dublin. But serving incomprehensible, and sometimes abusive, drunks late at night was no more exciting to me than the painting and hardware businesses had been. Joe was fairly friendly with Pat Grace who purportedly had the Irish franchise and the *secret* formula for KFC, and he still had the equipment from that venture. It was once again necessary to serve food at the Curracloe venue, but this wasn't a problem as we had the alleged recipe for the KFC (Kentucky Fried Chicken).

But we ran into difficulties on the opening Friday night of a bank holiday weekend, with the band not arriving on time, the sound system being dodgy and other problems.

We managed to iron out those matters but resolved that there would be no screw-ups in the future. On the following weekend, totally confident that everything was in hand, Joe and I went to the Farmers Kitchen beyond Wexford town on the Rosslare Road to have a celebratory meal ahead of the gig. Back at the venue, we found everything perfect, the band had arrived, the sound was perfect, and the place was full of paying customers, so we thought nothing could go wrong. Until there was a power cut.

There's a long-standing show-business tradition that says *the show must go on*, and inspired by that philosophy we decided to improvise. That night's bill included a Dublin comedian called the Red Flame, so we positioned him standing in the middle of the dance area, while Joe and I stood either side of him holding up a candle each! So the show did go on, and it was a huge success, especially after power was restored.

For those gigs, we booked commercial acts like the Dublin City Ramblers and Brendan Grace and learned that, contrary to our expectations, the high-priced acts always gave us far bigger profits than acts we booked for lesser fees. Then, one night came another major problem. With the place full, when the chicken for the meals arrived we noticed it was off, unusable and inedible. In somewhat of a panic, but determined not to be defeated, I sent a chap off to buy me 15 pounds of sausages and using the afore-mentioned KFC recipe, we invented the Kentucky Fried Sausage. Unfortunately, I forgot to tell Colonel Saunders. It could have been an international winner! Yes, *the show must go on*, and it did.

These ventures helped pay the rent and feed a family of four. But, round about then, my wife Cathy developed health problems which resulted in extended stays in hospital. Those problems continued and left me with few options of how to earn money and care for the children. So at weekends, I'd put Suzanne into a Cottage Home, a semi-orphanage in South County Dublin, and as soon as it was practical, probably around 1979, I'd take Jonathan into the Lombard Street office with me to look after him as best I could.

Luckily, the recording studio there was equipped with a Space Invaders machine. As it happens, Jonathan grew up to be an expert around computers and has worked successfully within the computer industry. I've often wondered if the seeds of that career were originally sown in his early years at the office. Either way, Space Invaders proved to be a great way of keeping him occupied while Deke and I got on with our work.

Scoff Record's first single was by a band called Square Meal which featured Steve Belton, a still active and much-admired guitarist. It came out in 1979, the same year U2 released their first record, so there was definitely something stirring rock-wise in Ireland. The punk movement encouraged rock musicians to avoid the major labels and make their own records on their own labels or those of their mates. There was a tremendous sense of freedom and energy sparked by the punk attitude which advocated less of an emphasis on musicianship and more on the attitude or political stance an act adopted.

Although not a punk band as such, U2 were undoubtedly influenced by the Punk ethos.

Punks took a fresh approach to song structure, and normal record production values went out the window and probably broke the window on the way! They looked askance at the music industry establishment and had little interest in, or knowledge of, the workings of an industry that some of them wanted to destroy! That said all those I met wanted to have records out, get played on the radio, be talked about in the media, do lots of gigs and make money, so there was an inherent contradiction at work with some of them. In one sense, behind it all, they were no different than many of the artists they criticized. Punk had taken root in Ireland as it had elsewhere, especially in the UK. But, we at Scoff had little contact with the UK market, partly because of the appalling Irish telephone service at the time, (it could take up to three years to get a landline) and the prohibitive cost of travel was another factor. We had some contact with indie labels like Rough Trade but it was hard to tie anything down from back home in Dublin.

The confrontational punk ethos was admirably displayed by The Boomtown Rats, The Sex Pistols and others, and it rubbed off on all of us to some degree, including myself. Back when I was Stepaside's manager I'd booked them into Dingwalls (a prestigious London venue), and was confronted by this London git making fun of the band's name-

'What's it mean?' he said in his sneering Cockney accent, 'Is it Irish for something?' To which I snarled back, 'Yeah, it's Irish for get out of my fuckin' way!' Yes, I was a rebel even back then.

Although I built up very positive relationships with many English people, it wasn't uncommon in that era to run into such occasional bouts of anti-Irishness both in England and at home. For instance, I went to the soundcheck for a *Showaddywaddy* concert in the National Stadium which had undergone a recent refurbishment that included some new tiles on the ceiling. In the process of setting up the band's gear, their English road crew requested a tall stepladder. An old codger who was a member of the Stadium staff duly brought over a 22-foot ladder and the crew shimmied up and started pushing out the new tiles to allow them to do what they wanted to do with their cables.

The staff guy shouted up to him, 'Hey, they're new tiles. You can't touch them!'

To which one of the English guys replied in a sneering tone, 'What's that's, Paddy? I don't understand Irish, ha, ha, ha!' and with that, he resumed moving the tiles. Now the old codger wasn't going to be treated so dismissively and so he casually approached and took the ladder away, leaving the mouthy crew stranded aloft. When the English guys spotted this they were quite alarmed. 'Hey, Paddy, what are you doing with that ladder?' one of them shouted.

The staff guy casually looked up and replied, 'What's that you're saying? I don't understand English!'...Boom, Boom!

Thankfully, those episodes were few and far between, and eventually became a rarity, but it stays with me as a fine example of spontaneous Irish humour in the face of a racist kind of stupidity.

Although no longer involved with The Time Machine, I was still running gigs in The Sportsman's, including *Scoff Nights* featuring our label signings and special guests that included the aforementioned Mr. Geldof as a solo artist. It was a great way of marketing our acts which in Ireland was extremely difficult and cost money we didn't have. *Hot Press* started in 1977, and 2FM, then called RTE Radio 2, had arrived to give us a more progressive diet of rock and pop music and quickly became essential outlets for getting the music and the acts exposed.

There was a growing sense of an important rock market in Ireland, even if it was still a minority interest. Radio 2 had DJs like Dave Fanning, Marty Whelan, Jimmy Greeley, Ronan Collins, Pat Kenny and Jim O'Neill who were as supportive as they could be, and I spent a lot of time *schmoozing* with some of the presenters who frequented Madigan's in Donnybrook, then affectionately known as RTE 3. In fact, *Hot Press* had the good sense to award me their coveted Ligger* of the Year Award in 1977 for my enthusiastic attendance at receptions and launches. I'd turn up at the opening of an envelope or a phone box if I thought I might meet a DJ who'd play our music.

Deke, with his musical background, operated mainly as the producer* and I looked after record & publishing contracts and admin. Derek Teeling also contributed and, amongst other things, brought us our first record with Square Meal who he managed. Always keen to learn from my mistakes, I'd taken the experience of losing Stepaside to Jim Hand to heart, and had proper contracts drawn up to cover all our dealings with Scoff artists or Dark Fox songwriters. Not that it solved all the problems. Sometimes the contracts themselves can cause problems! For example, we were negotiating with one particular act and I was starting to take them through the contract. When I read the section that has the act's name followed by the standard term 'The Artist hereby agrees', one of them objected on the basis that it, 'wasn't cool' to be referred to as 'the Artist', Oh dear! That conversation ended right there!

Looking back, we were enthusiastic amateurs making no money but dedicated to the cause, and I reckon we released about 45 singles and maybe 8 or 9 albums, with The Atrix and The Rhythm Kings probably being the most successful acts in commercial and profile terms.

The Atrix name was an adaptation of the word, 'theatrics', as they had theatrical leanings. They were quite an avant-garde outfit and fit in with what was happening in the mid-seventies, both with labels like Stiff Records whose catchy slogan was, 'If it ain't Stiff, it ain't worth a fuck', or Rough Trade in the UK and Ireland, and they inadvertently supplied me with a funny story from back then. Over a drink in The Bailey in Dublin the late John Borrowman, the band's guitarist and vocalist, very excitedly told me about their plans for a Christmas single he'd just written. When I asked him if he had a title for it he told me it was – 'Slaughtered and Maimed'. Slightly, eh, shocked I said, 'You want to release a Christmas single called 'Slaughtered and Maimed'?' He continued to express his enthusiasm and asked what I thought. I said, 'Tell me, John, it is in the key of fuckin' H demented?' But that was all part of the madness of rock back then.

Scoff also released two compilation albums, one called *Stock In Trade* and the other *Vinyl Verdict*. The latter included a track by The End who featured Tom Dunne on lead vocals, later to achieve fame with the band Something Happens! And who is now also a fine radio presenter.

At one point I decided we should make a play for the enormous American market, convinced that some Scoff acts, especially The Atrix and Tony

Coughlan (aka Koklin), might be better suited to the US market than elsewhere. So, in 1979 I set a plan in motion to visit some independent record labels out there with a view to persuading them to license* Scoff tracks for their own labels. Unfortunately, there was one major drawback, we'd no money! In those days (pre-Ryanair & mass air travel) flying across the Atlantic was an expensive and exotic experience. I reckoned I'd need at least two thousand quid to fund my trip… *How the fuck was I gonna do that?*

Then I hit on it! At the time a guy called Bobby Coffey, who was a good customer with Home & Garden, had a stall in Dun Laoghaire Shopping Centre. He made and sold wood carvings of Irish scenes which struck me as quite unique. It also occurred to me they might do very nicely in the US, and if I was smart, I could use these artworks to pay for my trip to LA.

So I offered to buy £500 worth of his carvings which I shipped to the *Coras Trachtala*/Irish Export Board office in New York, this was a state-funded organization intended to assist Irish enterprises to crack foreign markets. They then set up an exhibition of these carvings for me and invited the cream of Irish-American society to the viewing, and I managed to sell them all! I cleared about two and a half grand which paid for my entire trip, and I brought Cathy, Suzanne and Jonathan with me. Cathy's married sister was living in New York then, and she and her husband generously invited us to stay with them. So, my only outlay was for flights and out of pocket expenses. I was still only 29 and this was my very first trip to the States but I was growing in confidence. A combination of necessity and business creativity has often led me to find such angles and work them to my benefit.

I still have a photo of me in New York with the Twin Towers in the background. From New York, I flew to Los Angeles where my cousin, Father Jack Beattie, a Catholic priest, lived, and where I'd set up meetings with several suitable record labels and publishing companies I'd studiously checked out as part of my prep for the trip.

What I wasn't prepared for was the size of L.A. This being my first visit I'd assumed it might be only a little bigger than Dublin, so I'd foolishly set up three meetings for the morning and three for the afternoon. This turned out to be more than I could physically get to, despite the fact that Father Jack had kindly given me the use of his car.

1979 Johnny and The Twin Towers

One of my first appointments was with Shapiro Bernstein, the well-known publishing company then based in the Charlie Chaplin Studios on La Brea Avenue. Driving along the freeway I spotted the off-ramp indicating, 'La Brea Avenue' and confidently headed that way. I pulled into a gas station and told the assistant I was looking for the Charlie Chaplin Studios, hoping he could direct me. When he looked at me quite puzzled I told him the studios were on La Brea Avenue. He looked at me and said, 'Mister, La Brea Avenue is 21 miles long, do you think I know every freakin' office along it?'

Nothing concrete came of that visit in terms of the record labels, but I built up a number of contacts which proved useful later, especially given the fact that music industry activities are often based on personal inter-action.

In 1979, I got involved in *Just For Kicks,* the first album compilation of Irish rock bands, which included tracks by U2, The Atrix, Berlin and others, with sleeve-notes by Dave Fanning. I used that record to set up another music publishing company, Foxrock Music Productions. That, now rare and legendary vinyl recording was, I believe, one of the first ever Irish rock compilation records. It also contained in the sleeve notes...

'Yis are too loud... Yis are too dear ... and Yis won't play here again'.

A response we attributed to the reaction of ballroom owners to rock musicians and which just about summed up the attitude of the showband-dominated establishment to Irish rock bands. Mind you it must also be acknowledged that the showbands contained many superb musicians, including Rory Gallagher, who'd been with The Fontana Showband, and Van Morrison with The Monarchs.

Speaking of Rory reminds me of an incident during one of my absences from the family home. I'd developed a platonic friendship with Myra Azzopardi who did PR work for Polygram Records in their Dublin office from 1978 to 1981.

By coincidence, she moved into the steward's lodge on the avenue up to Woodbrook Golf Club and she had a room available there. This suited me fine, as it meant I was near the golf club and also not far from my family. Through Myra, I became friendly with the Irish musician Joe O'Donnell who was part of the Polygram stable of artists and was managed by Donal Gallagher, brother of Rory. He'd released an album called *Gaodhal's Vision* and I was confident I could look after him and his band full-time in some form of management capacity. Joe's band offered a kind of jazz/folk/rock sound and had a Canadian drummer, the magnificently named Theodore Thunder. I actually flew down to Cork to meet Donal, thinking I must have hit the big-time to be flying to meetings in Ireland, and he agreed to try me out for a gig Joe was doing at the Macroom festival that year. I met the band in Dublin and drove them to their hotel in Cork having arranged for their equipment to be sent by train and a local farmer to collect the gear with his tractor & trailer (van rental had yet to arrive in Macroom Co. Cork) from the local train station and deliver it to the rehearsal space.

But, when I turned up for the rehearsals the band members were lolling around doing nothing because only half the equipment had arrived. So I drove back to the station to find out what had happened, but on the way, I spotted the trailer with the gear on it outside a house. In a fury, I knocked on the door to ask what was going on and was told by a lady who opened the door that the driver was having lunch.

'Having lunch?' I spluttered, 'There's no fuckin' lunch in rock'n'roll!'

So that's how the music business works, you do whatever it takes to make the show happen, and letting a trivial matter, like lunch, screw it up just isn't on! The live music industry, in particular, has little tolerance for people not delivering, and that saying 'the show must go on' is no idle one.

Years later, and on the other side of the world, a guitar technician with Clannad who was suffering from a hangover handed the band's Pol Brennan an out-of-tune guitar on-stage during a show at a prestigious gig in Sydney, Australia. I was there in the audience and nearly died when the band had to stop mid song. He was fired instantly by the Tour Manager* and on the next flight back to the UK. After all, members of a paying audience are entitled to a 100% professional performance. Besides, if there's a problem with tuning, the audience are more likely to blame the act, not the technicians, many of whose existence or duties go unnoticed. And there were even more lessons to be learned as time went on and I burrowed deeper into the business they call *Show*.

I stayed with Scoff Records until 1981 when I was tempted to embark on what turned out to be a much bigger and more profitable venture, leaving Deke with complete ownership of Scoff Records and Dark Fox Catalogues. The label has been openly acknowledged as having made a serious contribution to the development of the indie ethos in Irish rock music as well as encouraging musicians towards having a more independent and self-reliant approach to their music careers. That contribution has been honoured in countless books, articles and documentaries detailing the growth of rock music in Ireland, something I'm very proud of.

But, it was time to move on......

Chapter Five

MUSIC PUBLISHING XPLAINED

I t all starts with a song…

Every day there are thousands of songs written. In my lifetime (forgive the pun) I must have listened to many, many thousands of songs with a view to signing the song (and therefore the writer) to a publishing deal. So at this point it might be useful to expand a little on what music publishing actually is and what exactly a music publisher does, which is a question I've been asked all my professional life. I like to simplify the answer by saying that a music publisher is a manager of songs…

The bottom line role of a publisher is to maximise the earning potential for both the songwriter and the publisher of the songs that are contracted to the publishing company in question. It's very much a background job, but a vital service to the songwriter.

First off, it has nothing to do with the kind of publishing we associate with newspapers and magazines or publishing a book. Music publishing actually began in the mid 1800's in Germany. But without getting too technical and boring you, dear reader, I'm going to skip to the origins in the UK, back in the 1900's. These were the days of Music Halls, Vaudeville, and Variety Shows which were the most popular form of public entertainment of those times. This was before the invention of the radio and back then, the role of music publishing was relatively straightforward. Songwriters would approach a music publisher for a deal, whereby the publisher would have a song's music

(&/or lyrics) notated and ascribed onto paper, which was printed, and sold to the public. These printed copies were known as *Sheet Music.*

In Britain, for example, music publishing companies were largely congregated in and around Denmark Street in London which was derisively known as Tin Pan Alley. The street, just off the Tottenham Court Road, is no more than about 500 yards long, but even today is littered with music shops and some studios. In fact, I think some early Rolling Stones recordings were made at No. 4 where the Regent Sound Studios were. So even though many of the music publishers have moved out, it still retains a link with music.

In the Tin Pan Alley days, songwriters would call around to the various music publishers trying to sell their songs. They were often confronted by what we'd call bouncers today, and some of them would actually sing or whistle their songs to the bouncers in order to convince them to let them through to a music publisher. Sometime later they'd call back and, according to music industry legend, if the bouncers could whistle one of their songs it meant it had passed what they called, '*the old Grey's whistle test*', later the term used as a name for a popular 1970's BBC rock programme fronted by Whisperin' Bob Harris. Having passed the test they were then admitted to the sanctum of the music publisher.

The publisher would subsequently try to generate more money by calling around to the music halls and vaudeville palaces, for which London was particularly famous, where they'd try to persuade the performers to sing their signed songs.

The arrival of radio in the early 1900's was a game changer. Now, songwriters and publishers could earn money from the broadcasts of their works through this new invention. Likewise, the invention of gramophone records, which, every time a record is mechanically produced generates a further royalty to the songwriters, composers and music publishers for the sale of the CD or vinyl discs. We're now in the early years of the digital age and today, technology is all pervasive.

Apple introduced iTunes (a digital download store or shop) in 2003 quickly followed with iPods, iPad etc…which allowed for the dissemination of music via the internet to the general public. Apple's first iPhone made its debut in 2007. Soon, other Android devices came on the market. There is expected to be 2.5 billion smartphones in use by 2019 worldwide. The proliferation of these devices, which allow for downloading, streaming etc... of music, coupled with audio and visual platforms such as YouTube present a whole new and complicated set of challenges to the music publisher of today.

The myriad of new royalty formats and potential digital income opportunities has given rise to significant challenges to the modern-day music publisher, not least because technology has greatly outstripped legislation, and continues to do so almost on a daily basis. Coupled with the fact that copyright legislation can, and does, vary from territory to territory, not only does a professional publisher need to keep abreast of these developments, they also need to have a vast legal understanding of copyright, and its workings, in order to be able to negotiate complex sub-publishing agreements.

Music publishing is primarily based on the concept of 'Intellectual Property' which, contrary to what some people have written, is not something conjured up by the music business but is a concept recognised in law in most western countries and many other states. It means the creator of a piece of work (music, design, literature, art etc) is deemed to be the owner of that work so it can only be used under conditions laid down by the copyright owners.

So, for example, if you were to write a song, anyone who uses it is legally obliged to pay you, the copyright owner for its various usages. The writer or composer of the music can retain the copyright themselves or can assign the copyright in that song to another person or a music publishing company. Either way, whoever owns the copyright in the work must be remunerated by the user of that composition.

Since most songwriters don't have the time, resources or expertise in exploiting the commercial value in their songs, the general practice is for them to assign the rights to a music publisher or music publishing company on agreed contractual terms. The publisher, in turn, tries to generate income for those songs by a variety of means as previously touched on.

As music publishers might not be able to monitor the uses of the songs on a national or global level, there are collection agencies in every country that collect the income on behalf of the copyright owners and distribute it to them. There are generally two different agencies operating in parallel, one collecting money for the use of songs in public performance, radio, television etc (Public Performance Right) and another collecting from the use of songs in recordings and in a motion picture film (referred to as Mechanical Right).

Those collection agencies link into an international network via a reciprocal agreement whereby, if the system is working efficiently, money earned by an Irish song in, say, Australia is collected by the Australian collection society (APRA) which then filters the money back along a financial pipeline to the Irish collection agency (IMRO) who pass it along to the music publisher who in turn pays the songwriter according to the terms of their contract. And that's how an Irish songwriter like, say, Jimmy MacCarthy, could earn money for a song of his being played on a radio station in a foreign country, and how an international songwriter such as Bob Dylan earns money from having his songs played on Irish radio. Publishing income is a very important (and potentially very lucrative) income stream for songwriters and their publishers. Just think how often Sir Elton John's songs are played on radio around the world daily... Do you get the picture?

I won't claim the system always works perfectly, but it's probably as good as it can be, and was enormously improved by computerisation. The Directors of these collection societies, which we call Collective Management Organisations or CMO's for short are constantly monitoring and improving these distribution systems, and as a founder (and current) Director of the Irish society IMRO, I am very familiar with this work. Part of the music publisher's job is to monitor all payments so as to ensure, as much as he or she can, that the songwriters signed to them receive all the income they are legally entitled to. It's also important to remember that the copyright in a song runs out 70 years after the death of its last living composer.

At the risk of terrorising the unwary, the role of a music publisher is to exploit the songs and compositions assigned to him by the songwriters on their roster. Exploitation is a rather emotive term and is open to misunderstanding, but it has a legitimate usage in this context. In practical terms, it means trying to find ways of increasing both the publisher's and the songwriter's income for those songs being used in a number of commercial situations as I've already outlined.

Another part of the role is to ensure as much as one can that all uses of those songs have been paid for, and drawing up contracts that enable others to legally use a song under agreed terms. Although there was a time in the past when matters were handled through oral agreements and handshakes, my policy is now, *no contract, no phone-call,* (having learned my lesson from the Stepaside-Jim Hand debacle outlined earlier).

Sadly, it's not always possible to take people at their word, and there can be genuine misunderstandings as to what the agreed deal really is, so until the legalities are taken care of I will carry out no work on any song. Legal contracts between parties can be and are quite complex and generally something songwriters don't care to be bothered with, so they employ a publisher with sufficient knowledge to handle these matters on their behalf. As you will read in a later chapter the sub-publishing deal I negotiated for Evolving Music and Sony/ATV ran to over one hundred pages and took me the best part of six months to conclude.

Armed with the requisite contracts, a publisher usually has the legal right to enter into sub-publishing deals whereby a publisher, probably in another territory, is allowed take on the role of the main publisher in that territory provided such arrangements are legally permissible under the terms of the original songwriter contract. That contract law and copyright law can vary from country to country and can add another layer of problems and increase the workload. And there are other differences. For example, in the USA there are three Public Performance collection agencies, BMI, ASCAP and SESAC, all in competition with each other. Also in the USA, any premises less than 2,500 square feet doesn't need a music license, thanks to the power of the lobbyists who work on their behalf on Capitol Hill. There are other anomalies in the American system that can work against the interests of the lower-earning American songwriters, yet they never seem to protest and meekly accept a situation that some will argue actually steals money from them. Pity I wasn't born in the USA… I would've caused havoc!

Contracted songs must be registered with all relevant collection agencies, because doing so gives those agencies the right to collect money on behalf of those songs and songwriters. It is the responsibility of the music publisher to ensure that happens efficiently and make the necessary enquiries regarding any inaccuracy or delay.

As you might imagine, keeping track of an extensive catalogue of songs that might be in use all over the planet is a complicated and time-consuming task. So attention to detail is absolutely crucial. Millions have been lost for publishers and songwriters by the careless reading of contracts or a lack of clear understanding of what key clauses might entail.

Aware of the money that can be amassed through songwriting, I'm regularly amazed whenever I observe the casual approach, bordering on indifference, that writers sometimes have towards what can be a life-long income source for them. It's not uncommon for me to be contacted by a songwriter who is seeking advice about his publishing contract. I usually tell them I'll happily have a look over it, but they should consult an experienced music industry lawyer before they sign it. Often having looked at the contract and seeing that it's not great from the writers' point of view I'd advise them not to sign the document only to discover they've already signed it, sometimes three or four years previously! Sadly, it's often the musicians and songwriters who pay the least attention to these matters and who later tend to complain the loudest because they didn't do as well financially from their careers as they believe they should have.

I recall one very well known Irish songwriter, in the middle of a business meeting he'd arranged with me, throwing me off my stride by asking me if I ever contemplated a lake. This, as you might imagine, had nothing to do with the matter we were discussing. I think what he was trying to say was that as a creative artiste, he had the sensitivity and moral superiority to think beyond the merely financial, whereas plebs like me couldn't rise to such exalted thinking. But, he was perhaps forgetting if we all thought about lakes all the time, no gigs would be promoted, and no records would be made or marketed. Indeed, no songs would be written, and he wouldn't make the kind of money he was very keen to make. For those who aren't interested in the more detailed explanations, I tell the following anecdote to explain the basic principles of music publishing:

A woman discovers her tap isn't working and she calls a plumber. The plumber arrives and finds that to be the case, and no matter how much he turns the tap on, no water comes out.

So he takes a large wrench out of his tool-bag and begins to trace the pipe back along the wall and into the next room, and then gently hits the pipe twice at a particular spot.

'Try that now missus,' says the plumber suggesting the woman tries the tap again.

She does so, and water immediately gushes out.

Delighted to have her problem solved, she asks the plumber,' How much do I owe you?'

He says, 'That'll be £37.50, Ma'am.'

She's aghast. '£37.50? Just for tapping on that pipe twice?'

The plumber shakes his head and says, 'No, no, Ma'am. It's £2.50 for tapping the pipe, and £35 for knowing where to tap it.'

In a way, that's what a publisher does. He must know where the money is in the pipeline and must make sure it comes out at his end. It's probably no coincidence that we often refer to such money as – 'being in the pipeline' or 'pipe-line income'.

The percentage deal between a publisher and a songwriter, and between one publisher and a sub-publisher can vary depending on the usual factors that govern business negotiations. Between songwriter and publisher, it can range from 50/50 to 70/30 or 80/20 or even higher, in favour of the writer. It can even go to 100/0 in favour of the writer, as I suspect it does for songwriters of the calibre of Paul McCartney or Stevie Wonder. Of course, people might wonder why a publisher might be happy with a 0% share, but contracts are usually structured so that money is paid out to writer clients maybe 6/9 months in arrears, so the publisher has the money to invest or earn interest on until it's paid over.

When a publisher signs a deal with a writer it's important for both parties to understand the dynamics of the arrangement. It's a little bit like a marriage.

You've committed to trust each other as you work together. The publisher may make some suggestions as to how the song might be improved from a commercial sense by say, tweaking a lyric or changing a chord or altering the structure of the song. Remember, the publisher is a professional listener and will always be looking to improve or enhance the work to maximise the experience that the public will hear, after all they'll be the ultimate deciders as to whether a song will be commercially successful. Often, the songwriter's ego might be offended by the publisher's suggestions and both parties must be able to work through those difficulties. I've often heard myself remark that sometimes being a publisher is like being a cross between a paralegal and a night nurse. But, hey! It goes with the territory.

That's the nuts and bolts of it, and it all works very logically, but deciding what songs to sign is a more complex matter, especially given the likelihood of having to put time, money and other resources behind them. In the first place, assessing the commercial potential of any song is a very subjective experience, one that can alter depending on your mood, the time of day, the company you're with, the reason you're listening to the song in the first place, the quality of the recording and performance. Most of us in the industry have probably had situations where a song we thought we didn't like suddenly seems very appealing, just as the reverse happens, and it's often hard to pin down exactly why this happens. I can verify that from personal experience.

In 1991 the American band Extreme had a hit with a song called 'More Than Words'. It was a big international hit and was played countless times on Irish radio as it was elsewhere around the globe. But, try as I might, I couldn't quite get it. Sure, I thought it was ok, but surely not that great a song? Years later I attended a Michael Buble concert in Dublin and was invited to the after-show party. At some point, Michael and some of his band members decided to give us an impromptu a cappella performance and the song they chose was, 'More Than Words'. This rendition blew me away, as the saying goes. For reasons I can't explain the song made sense this time around, and I could now understand why it had been such a hit. Music is subjective!

But, the history of the music industry is littered with such emotions, so

I'm in good company. When Queen played their new manager John Reid their nearly six-minute long recording of their bombastic pomp-rock masterpiece, 'Bohemian Rhapsody' and suggested it as their new single he was flabbergasted, convinced it was far too long for radio airplay. Their record company EMI were equally sceptical. But, the band refused to shorten their grandiosely operatic four-part epic and passed a pre-release copy of the single to their friend and Capital Radio DJ Kenny Everett just for his own private collection. But, Everett was so taken by the recording he broke his promise, played it on the radio fourteen times over two days and the subsequent response jammed Capital's switchboard. The record became a multi-million seller and is often voted as one of the best singles of all time.

I should also emphasise that music publishers are looking for different things than say, a record company. The latter, when considering signing an act, will take into consideration their image and age, their personalities, stage presence and musical ability, their marketability and various other factors. The music publisher focuses exclusively on the song and tries to assess whether it can generate revenue or not.

Whenever I receive a demo from a songwriter and manage to find time to listen to it, the first thing I need to clarify is what are the songwriter's intentions? Are they hoping to carve a career as a singer-songwriter, are they looking to get the songs covered by other artists, or used in films or television commercials or what?

After all, there's no point in me chasing advertising agencies to get a song used in a TV commercial if that is definitely not the direction the writer wants to head in.

The art of being a (successful) music publisher requires a number of key elements. First and most obvious is the ability to recognise a good song and its ability to earn money. This can't really be taught. You either have ears (as they say in the trade) or you don't. Secondly, a publisher must be an expert in the whole area of copyright law which can and generally does differ from territory to territory. It's also imperative that the publisher knows all the ways a song can be exploited, whether it is likely to appeal to radio listeners and therefore generate revenue and how to secure the best deal from said exploitation.

A lot of the work is administrative and can be quite tedious, but this, and attention to detail is paramount. When I wrote my brief informational booklet, *The Need to Know Guide to Music Publishing*, twenty years ago (doesn't time fly when you're having fun?) I used a quote from Ernest Roth taken from *This Business of Music*, a very worthwhile read for anyone aspiring to a career in the business:

'*Among all of those who live for and off (sic) music, the music publisher plays the most ambiguous part. He stands at the crossroads of art and commerce, where enthusiasm for art and business sense meet or miss each other: between artistic obsession and commercial acumen, promoting the art and translating it into good money. Composers expect from him both fame and fortune.*'

Quite!!

Chapter Six

CLANNAD'S GAME

Towards the end of the natural shelf life of Scoff Records, an opportunity arose with the emerging international band Clannad. The Clannad connection arose through a friendship that had developed with Dave Kavanagh, their manager from Dublin. Dave was the Entertainments Officer in UCD, and we'd met regularly on the rock circuit while I was managing Time Machine and he had Sacre Bleu, a lively Dublin rock band, and they were both often paired on the same bill. With Charlie McNally, Dave had also promoted a concert by American blues-rock outfit Canned Heat at the National Stadium in 1976. But I first met Dave when they were promoting a concert by Chuck Berry at the National Stadium in the mid-70s.

I learned that encores could cost money, because when Chuck finished his set and came backstage covered in sweat, the capacity crowd in the stadium were going crazy and roaring for more, Dave tried to encourage him to go back on for the standard encore. Chuck replied 'Listen, Honkey, encores cost money,' and insisted he'd only do an encore if he was paid another $500. Dave went away, came back, and handed Chuck 250 Irish pounds (our currency at the time which was probably worth less in Dollars.) Looking at these strange notes, Chuck said, 'What's that, honky?' Dave said, 'It's $500,' and Chuck played the encore. Dave also worked with the Chieftains and was the agent for The Boomtown Rats and U2 and had a deep knowledge of the international aspect of the music industry that few others in Ireland had at that time.

The name Clannad comes from the amalgam of *Clann* (which means family in Gaelic) *As* (from) and *Dore* (the townland in Donegal where they were born). They're a family band consisting of Maire (pronounced Moya) and her brothers Ciaran and Paul Brennan, together with their twin uncles Padraig and Noel Duggan. This, I believe, is where they get their unique family sound which has captivated audiences globally.

When Dave took on the management of Clannad in 1980 he invited me to listen to a recording of a song in his flat in Dun Laoghaire. He played me a track and asked what I thought of it. 'Dave', I said, 'that song will either be a huge hit or it'll disappear without a trace.' That song was the 'Theme From Harry's Game'. The recording was to go on to huge international success, appearing in the charts all over the world. But before that could happen, Dave had a crucial meeting in London in relation to Clannad signing an international record deal with RCA Records.

Dave called me the night before he was due to go to London for the important meeting with RCA records-

'Johnny, they're going to ask me about publishing, and I know nothing about publishing. Tell me how publishing actually works.'

I said, 'Jesus, Dave, you want me to explain music publishing to you in three minutes?'

He said, 'Yeah.'

So I said- 'It's too complicated for that. But here's my advice. Your best bet is to remember these three words I'm going to give you for that meeting and say them if or when they ask about publishing.'

'Three words?'

'Yes, three words. When they bring up the subject tell them you want to *retain the copyright*. Have you got those three words, *retain the copyright?*'

I made him repeat 'retain the copyright' to make sure he'd got it. Sure enough, the London meeting went according to plan, and Dave used the three words I'd given him.

When he returned to Dublin Dave asked me to explain what retain the copyright meant, and that's how he invited me to form Clannad Music Ltd and to run it for him full-time in his office. It was the start of a very rewarding business and personal relationship that continued until he died in April 2018. He was one of my closest friends for 43 years, a mentor and a wonderful man.

The first 'Clannad' office was in Novara Avenue, Bray, rented from another publisher, Peter Bardon. We were housed in a large room. Dave and I shared a desk and we called the band's management company, Upfront Management, with Dave as MD and me as Business Affairs Director. I was paid a small retainer, with expectations of serious earnings down the line. Apart from running Clannad's publishing affairs, I would also handle the management office admin which really appealed to me as my forte has always been attention to detail, whereas Dave had a more creative approach, doing deals and working on his unique vision for the band's international development. I learned so much from Dave watching his brilliant professional management style. He was the best manager I'd ever seen and indeed probably ever will see.

I've never been a huge fan of Irish traditional music, but I loved Clannad's family sound and their willingness to experiment and take the music to places it had never been before, using synthesizers and multi-tracking and creating those marvelous soundscapes behind Moya Brennan's wonderful voice.

I admired their ambition in not wanting to be just another very good Irish traditional band on the Irish folk circuit. We had plenty of those to keep us fully stocked for a while. Instead, Clannad's plans, devised in conjunction with Dave, were to make Irish traditional music relevant to the modern world, and all the band members and management were on the same page with that goal.

My real office work began when Leon Brennan, a brother of Clannad members' Moya, Pol and Ciaran, arrived into the office carrying a large black sack of paper filled to the brim which he emptied on the floor. 'What's that?' I said and Leon replied, 'That's all the band's receipts for the last year for you to sort out.'

In that office, I saw just how a smart manager works. Guinness offered Dave a very substantial fee to sponsor a tour of Australia involving Clannad, Brendan Grace and De Danann, with each act headlining on a rota basis.

Given that we were only a little above destitute level, I was amazed when he turned it down. On hearing the proposed deal, I said, 'What the fuck Dave, we've no money?' But he explained to me it would be a wrong career move for Clannad, and he was confident that more attractive opportunities would come later, which they did. He had a vision as to how he wanted to steer the band's career, the specific markets he was aiming at, and the image he wanted the band to develop. He could see the long-term view and was prepared to make short-term sacrifices as he encouraged Clannad from being a parochial folk band with the whole folky/hippy vibe into an internationally-acclaimed, sophisticated Celtic/New Age act. The band understood that vision and exemplified it totally.

1985 Backstage with Clannad at the Olympia, Dublin

Dave's background was in rock music, so he could think internationally in a way few Irish managers of the day could, and he had the foresight that showband managers rarely had. Most of the latter only seemed to think ahead as far as the next gig and rarely, if ever, even thought of looking at the global picture. Dave was not likely to make that mistake, and his plans soon turned into success. We used to write our own Press Releases marveling at Clannad's unique sound and it'd amuse us when our own words would appear in a record company blurb and then would very often appear in the music industry papers. But the band DID have a unique sound and their reputation started to take off around the world following the 'Harry's Game' hit.

We kept the Bray office for a few years before moving down to Sir John Rogerson's Quay beside the River Liffey in Dublin where television producers Conor MacAnally and Bill Hughes also had offices. Clannad were by then enjoying success in the USA and elsewhere around the globe, and there were advantages in being closer to the heart of Dublin City.

We were also close to the Windmill Lane Studios which at the time were regarded as one of the best studios in the world, and where *U2* recorded most of their earliest recordings. Clannad's growing international popularity paralleled the international success of U2, and Dave was very friendly with their manager Paul McGuinness whose office just happened to be near ours too. So, the area was becoming a sort of music industry hub and somewhat of a tourist attraction as fans from all over the globe started flocking to Dublin to check out the city that had spawned U2.

The wall at the Windmill Lane Studio became an attraction in its own right, as fans scrawled their messages to the band and to each other.

Various members of both U2 and Clannad, as well as their management and staff, often met for drinks or a sandwich in the nearby Dockers pub. They could be joined by others, including the likes of Elvis Costello and Sinead O'Connor or any of the acts who might be visiting Windmill Lane. I recall meeting Chris Blackwell, owner of Island Records, to whom U2 were signed there on several occasions.

Soon the pub also become a magnet for over-enthusiastic fans keen to meet, or even clap eyes on, their musical heroes, and there were many occasions when it was necessary for somebody, sometimes myself, to 'protect' Bono and members of U2 from being interrupted on a Friday night after work having a pint.

Incidentally, it was also in that bar, albeit some years later, that I first encountered the term e-mail when I heard a reference to one by Joe O'Herlihy, U2's sound engineer. Meanwhile, a close friendship was being formed between Clannad, especially singer Moya, and U2. Bono was a big Clannad fan, admitting when he first heard 'Harry's Game' he nearly crashed the car he was driving, so enthralled was he by this fresh, magical Celtic sound with lyrics in the Irish language.

Around 1982/3 a U2 concert was planned for Radio City in New York with Clannad as support act. Unfortunately, the concert was cancelled for reasons I can't remember, but I still have a poster advertising the gig. U2 were generously supportive of Clannad and sometimes played recorded music by Clannad to the expectant audience before they took to the stage.

In 1985 a plan was hatched (in the Dockers naturally) for Bono to join forces with Clannad to provide guest vocals on the track, 'In A Lifetime', a song written by Ciaran and Pol Brennan. It was recorded in Windmill Lane Studios as part of the new Clannad album *Macalla*. In fact, I was present in the studio for the recording and actually took some photos of Bono, Ciaran & Moya working up the track. Unfortunately, I later lost the camera! (Imagine what I could get for those photos today on eBay LOL!) It's important to note this collaboration came about quite organically through mutual admiration, whereas many of today's musical collaborations are contrived by the marketing departments of record companies to help boost the profiles of one or both of the artists involved. At this point, neither U2 nor Clannad needed to employ such a tactic, as both were already established international acts in their own right. When 'In A Lifetime', was later released as a Clannad single featuring Bono it became a substantial global hit and indeed inspired the title of this book, 30 years later!

Clannad had an unwritten policy of doing as many photo shoots and recording as much video footage as possible in their native Donegal, and I went with them and Bono to shoot the video for 'In A Lifetime'. We stayed in a hotel called Ostan Gweedore in the village of Gweedore, and I was having breakfast with Moya and Bono and others when I saw first-hand how intrusive fame can be. Bono was about to drink a mouthful of orange juice when an excited waitress interrupted to ask him to sign an autograph. Bono was totally unfazed by this inconvenience, calmly put the glass down and signed something for her. This was typical of Bono who, as I'd noticed with the other members of the band, was always polite and patient with his fans, no matter how inconvenient, and always took a professional and business-like approach to his work.

1985 Leon Brennan, Clannad Office

But it struck me that even while having breakfast at 7am in the morning in a remote Irish hotel there was no escape from the gaze of the demanding public. Fame is something you really need to want and few realise the sacrifices it demands.

Although I was generally office based, I sometimes got the opportunity to work with the band on the road, and this time at the far end of the world, when Dave appointed a new tour manager* Phil McDonald, an Englishman, in time for their first tour of Australia. It seemed unfair to Dave to land the new guy with the responsibility of a six-week tour, while venturing into what he expected would be a lucrative market for the family band who also spoke to each other in Gaelic, which was their first language.

Dave said, 'Johnny you've got to go to Australia with the guys,'

I said, 'But Dave, they leave in four days!'

Not exactly a lot of notice to travel to the other side of the world, but I saw his point as I was already very familiar with the band members and their personalities and sensitivities. Sometimes you end up being a referee trying to settle disputes between family members. But then I had my own family dispute to take care of. Cathy and I had split by then and I had a new girlfriend, Jenny, who strongly objected to (I believe the words she used were fuckin' off to) me going to Australia for six weeks. I tried to explain it was actually my job, but she didn't seem to get it. Naturally, I went anyway. Who, in their right mind would turn down an all-expenses-paid working trip to every major city in Australia?

1988 Phil McDonnell and Murty, Australia

It's a long flight from Dublin and when we arrived we checked into the Sebel Townhouse, which was known as a rock'n'roll hotel, near Sydney harbour. Not being able to sleep because of jet lag, I got up in the middle of the night to go for a walk. At reception, I said to the night porter, 'If I go outside the front door I'll be lost'. He said,' If you turn right you'll arrive at the harbour, but if you turn left you'll arrive in King's Cross, an area full of nightlife.' First I'd heard of it back then, so I turned left! It was 4 am on my first night in Oz.

The area I walked into was lit up like Las Vegas, with hookers, pimps, drug addicts, drug dealers, tramps, derelicts, all human life was there. It reminded me of the Tom Waits, '(Looking For) The Heart of Saturday Night'. And I'd found it, in Sydney. I loved it! One night in the bar of the Sebel I got chatting to a guy who ran the *Southern Cross Railway,* linking Sydney with Canberra and like an Australian equivalent of the Orient Express. The band's first gig happened to be the following Saturday night in

Canberra. It was sold out with the Irish ambassador to Australia due to attend.

So, I made a deal with the guy that Clannad would travel on the Southern Cross train for free in return for having photos taken of them getting on the train which he could then use for his own publicity purposes. This was fairly common practice, an arrangement that works for both parties. The train was all decked out in Victorian style. Travelling onboard we had the core members of the band, as well as musicians augmenting the line-up, some of whom liked a drink. With relative ease, they found the onboard bar and settled in for the journey. Pol Brennan, the guitar-playing member of the band, approached me. He was always very professional in his attitude. 'John,' he said (I knew I was in trouble when he called me John). 'Do you know where my brother Ciaran is?'

'Yes Paul', I replied,' He's at the bar having a drink'. (This was not unusual for musicians, believe me!).

1988 Ciaran Brennan, Clannad at the bar on the
Southern Cross Train to Canberra

He felt so strongly about this he demanded a band meeting on the spot to discuss it which was duly arranged between the five members of Clannad, Phil and myself. Pol then announced that, because his brother and some of the musicians were drinking at the bar, in his view we should cancel that night's gig. I reflected on this for a moment and said to him, 'Ok. So this is what you want me to do. I'm to phone Kavanagh in Dublin and advise him that you want to cancel Clannad's first ever Australian gig which the Irish Ambassador to Australia has had in his diary for weeks. We'll then have to inform the promoter who'll have to refund tickets for the show that's been sold-out for weeks. The promoter will most likely cancel any other concerts we've arranged with him for the rest of the tour and refuse to ever work with us again and also probably sue us for loss of earnings and damage to his reputation. You really think that's the best way to announce our first ever visit to Australia?'

Fortunately, common sense prevailed, but these are the issues a tour manager has to deal with when musicians don't think through the possible repercussions that follow from their knee-jerk reaction to something they don't approve of. But it's easy to understand how a band can virtually disappear into a bubble shared with a small number of people and that alters their view of what's going on outside. You can tour the entire continent and not actually see much of it other than the venue, the hotel and the inside of the tour bus, train, taxi or plane. The sense of unreality this creates can be exemplified by another story from the same tour. It's not unusual for a record company to entertain the band, management and key members of the crew when they arrive in a town. So, when we had a night off in Sydney the record company took about 20 of us to the very famous Doyle's Seafood Restaurant for a superb night. While crossing Sydney Bridge on the way back to our hotel I fell into a conversation with some of the band, and one of them asked me, 'Who was that record company who entertained us tonight?'

I said, 'BMG Records'.

He said, 'BMG?'

I said, 'Yes, BMG the label we're signed to.'

He said, 'Ah no, no, no, we're signed to RCA.'

'Look, BMG bought RCA a few years ago,' I told him, before adding, 'Who did you think would spend a few thousand quid entertaining twenty of us in one of the top restaurants in the country?'

'Well,' he said, 'it could have been EMI or maybe Sony'.

I looked at him. 'But why would they do that for a band not even signed to them?'

He said, 'Maybe for the craic, like.'

I don't know what planet he was on at the time, but a record company lavishing such hospitality on a band signed to another label is something I haven't come across on the planet I live on. In fact, it's the usual practice for the costs of such hospitality, plus a surcharge, to be subsequently deducted from the band's royalty income anyway. Thankfully, most of the madness takes place away from, or after, the gigs, and this tour was a terrific success. Clannad became a huge act in Australia, and New Zealand too. Probably the only real casualty was my relationship with Jenny, which didn't survive the trip!

Controlling expenditure on a tour can be another problem. On a UK tour, Phil came to me to raise just that concern. It was his duty to settle up hotel bills as we checked out, and he noticed the amounts were escalating. I examined the bills and discovered that before departing from a hotel some of the band would take with them whatever was left in the mini-bar in their rooms. When I asked them about this I discovered they thought all the drink was free, compliments of the hotel.

It was, and still is, quite common for artists to order limos or bottles of expensive champagne assuming the record company or somebody else was doing the paying, only to find when their royalty statements came through, these expenses were deducted from what was due to them. Of course, this was in the pre-computer days and at a time when there could be vagueness as to who was paying for what, not a problem that arises much these days!

My time with Clannad was a real education as I learned all about international copyright income as it might accrue from synchronization rights*, i.e. the use of music in television programmes and films. There were many highlights during my time with Clannad, some because we were moving from playing concerts at venues like the London Palladium to bigger arenas such as the Royal Albert Hall. The excitement of moving up to the next level is pretty contagious. But for me, the peak with Clannad was the band winning the BAFTA Award in March 1985 for Best Original TV Music for the series *Robin of Sherwood* (retitled *Robin Hood* in the USA). The awards ceremony was a formal affair in London's Grosvenor Hotel for which we hired the required number of dress suits. Unfortunately, when we changed into our finery we were one dickie bow short. Naturally, me not being a member of the band, I volunteered to hand mine over. That explains why the photos from that occasion show me in a white jacket and dress shirt with no dickie bow. All through the evening, people thought I was a waiter, (although nobody offered me any tips!).

1985 Clannad (with David Jason) winners of the Bafta award

Contrary to general assumptions, you go to these events unaware of whether you're going to win or not. All you know is that you've been short-listed. When I heard Clannad's name announced as the winners, it sparked an extraordinary adrenalin rush which is nigh on impossible to describe. To celebrate, we all went to Tramp nightclub, one of the trendiest nightclubs in London. During a hugely enjoyable evening, I was exchanging small talk with Freddie Mercury of Queen fame. He started making facial gestures at me, puckering his lips, the lot. This made me think he fancied me and thought I was gay too. Not being gay, I didn't respond, but have often wondered what would've happened had I taken an interest in his pretty obvious offer??

Later that night I also met Alex Higgins, the legendary Snooker player from Northern Ireland, who'd just recently lost a crucial match in a major tournament. I was still so high on the adrenalin rush I decided to explain to

Alex where he was going wrong, and how he could win more often. I'm sure my advice included telling him to control his drinking habit and was based on no knowledge whatsoever of a sport in which he was already a legend. But it shows how bloated with your own self-regard you can get with that adrenaline high. You're convinced you're completely correct and know it all and become most eager to impart your invaluable advice to the world. I was probably lucky Alex didn't ram one of his cues up my arse! Anyway, I don't think he heeded any of my 'advice', so no harm done.

Touring can become incredibly tedious, going from place to place and living out of a suitcase, so some madcap antics within the tour party personnel are fairly common. One such prank I remember well. On a visit to Paris, to pass the time in the hotel, myself and Phil, took the lift to the top floor and held it open. We moved a dinner table and chairs into the lift, complete with candles, food and a bottle of wine, and sat there eating and chatting nonchalantly as if it was something we did all the time. When people opened the lift doors on different floors, they looked at us with bemused expressions while we, never glancing at the shocked guests, just looked directly at each other and continued chatting. The hotel manager however, was not amused, so the prank didn't last too long. Many such jokes and events occurred (in those days), and as the showbiz maxim goes, 'what happens on tour stays on tour...' I'm keeping some of the more salacious stories for another book!

Ironically, the bigger Clannad became the more expensive it got to keep them on the road. Fans have expectations that you're growing and progressing to bigger and better things, but all that costs money in terms of stage production. The band's artistic ambitions saw their want for additional musicians on stage to augment their unique sound. Phil as tour manager, and I as Business Affairs manager, were both working on the budget for the World Tour in 1988 when Dave pointed out we needed to trim £25,000 from the expenditure. We spent days trying to reconfigure everything, putting all the gear into two trucks instead of three, and so on, looking for every possible area where we could cut costs. In the end we did it, and when I announced this to Dave in front of the band they said, 'Oh great, now we can get extra lights!' This'd be a fairly typical example of how musicians' aspirations and business practicalities often collide.

But I also have fond memories of the pioneering music they made. There were so many memorable live concerts in various parts of the world, and I especially liked their *Magical Ring* album. Not only does it contain the wonderful, 'Theme from Harry's Game', but also has 'I See Red' which is basically a pop song and on which they married pop and traditional sensibilities to create something uniquely modern. Another favourite of mine is *Legend* (the *Robin of Sherwood* Soundtrack). It came out in 1984 and had the hit single 'Robin (The Hooded Man)'. But the diehard fans thought they moved a step too far too soon when they did *Sirius*, although I liked it myself. It was more hard rock than the fans were used to, and had musicians of the calibre of Steve Perry of Journey, Bruce Hornsby and JD Souther appearing on the record.

Dave and I made another addition to the Upfront stable in the late 80s when we signed the Wexford band Cry Before Dawn for management and landed them a record deal with Sony Music. A funny incident I remember was when during an early Irish tour, we had them booked for a gig in a ballroom in Cork one Friday night and I decided to drive them down from Dublin in my car.

Unfortunately, when we got to Monasterevin in County Kildare the clutch in my car gave up. But I soon found a car dealer in the town and got the band to push the car down to the dealership. The owner was locking up his garage for the weekend. I explained my plight. I badly needed a car to get us to Cork. Unfortunately, the car man wasn't so keen to help, so I ended up 'making him an offer he couldn't refuse' as the saying goes, that if he didn't help by loaning me a car on the spot I would break into his gleaming showrooms and borrow one until Monday! So now he had a choice. He could either help me, and be free to enjoy his Friday night, or he'd have to stay here and keep an eye on us to protect his cars. He opted for the former, thankfully loaned us a car and we made the gig, but the incident proves when that old adage- 'the show must go on', takes hold, sometimes, you'll stop at nothing.

Working with Cry Before Dawn also gave me another insight into the way record company bosses think. We had two albums out on Sony, and a UK hit with the single, 'Witness For The World'. CBD were an extremely talented bunch of musicians, but Sony having invested a considerable pile of money in the band, and made several expensive promo videos, told us they were £750,000 down on their investment, and were thinking seriously about taking up the next option on the contract which would require a further injection of money.

1986 Cry Before Dawn in the Mean Fiddler

Round about that time their talent scouts had discovered a promising Scottish band called Deacon Blue, so their dilemma was either to continue with CBD and risk more investment, or sign the new guys. Either way was a risk, but they opted for the latter, and scored well over a dozen hit singles and heaps of album sales. Disappointed as I was for the CBD team, it'd be hard to argue in hindsight that Sony had picked the wrong option. Because, in reality, that's the way the music business works at the top end. Major record companies sign, say, ten bands and invest a fixed sum of money in each. One of the ten has the desired commercial success and they drop the other nine! It's as simple, or as some might say, cynical, as that. It's got fuck all to do with talent. In any event, talent is not enough! You also need luck and being in the right place at the right time with the right material.

That decision by Sony didn't help our income situation, and one day in

1990 I realized, having examined our accounts books, that the management company was actually losing money. So, I went to Dave and said, 'This operation has become too expensive, and you and me are the biggest expenses. So I reckon one of us will have to go, and I guess it won't be you.' Yes, it was me. I suppose you could say it was a kind of voluntary redundancy. I was 40 years of age, and I'd used my experience in Pop's business to paint myself into a corner!

Postscript

In July 2018 I was invited to Clannad's home-place in Gweedore, Co Donegal. The band were celebrating two events: The 50-year anniversary of the opening of Leo's Tavern, the world famous pub which was opened in 1968 by their parents Leo and Baba Brennan and where Clannad, and their sister Enya, began their singing careers. The band were also launching a new recording - *Turas 1980*, a live recording of a Clannad concert performed in Bremen, Germany in 1980.

The celebration of both events were held over three days and included gigs by not only Clannad themselves but guest appearances by the legendary 1960s icon Donovan, the original 1980s punk poet Hazel O'Connor, (whose song catalogue I administered for a number of years) as well as appearances by Daniel O'Donnell and Phil Coulter.

The Clannad performance that night brought back so many memories and they still sound as brilliant and pure as when I first saw them live some 37 years previously in 1981. The current Clannad line-up now includes Moya's daughter Aisling (bazooka and guitar) and son Paul (drums & percussion) who are extremely talented musicians in their own right, and thus ensure the legend of this family band will live on for future generations.

2018 Clannad, Leo's Tavern, Donegal

2016 Dave Kavanagh with son Luke and our mate,
Stephen Power, at the K Club

1986 Dave Kavanagh backstage

1985 Clannad, Moya Brennan's birthday with
Dave Kavangh at the London Palladium

Chapter Seven

FROM THE GULF WAR TO THE MUSIC POLICE

H aving moved out of Clannad's office and having no great plans in mind, I sent out a press release telling the music industry in Ireland I was available for whatever work anybody might like to put my way. That effort elicited no responses of any significance, apart from being offered a little consultancy work for Brian Molloy in the Lombard Street set-up. Just as I'd realised the painting and hardware business was not for me, I'd come to the conclusion that looking after artists and booking gigs wasn't a job I was cut out for either, especially as it required endless reams of patience, a quality I've never been over-burdened with. I became increasingly enthusiastic about developing my own music publishing operation. Having set up Dark Fox Music for Scoff in the 70s and Clannad Music Ltd for Dave & myself in the 80s, I decided to set up my own music publishing & management consultancy company and called it Covert Music Productions. Yes, you might be forgiven for thinking I had some kind of fox obsession!

On the domestic front matters had seriously deteriorated. The decline in Cathy's health, which began back in 1976, meant that she'd often undergo hospital treatment for up to 6 weeks at a time. I too was absent from the home for short periods as I tried to keep my own life together, and also because I found it difficult to cope with her problems. She suffered from, what is known today as, severe Bi-Polar disorder. I discovered the line between sanity and insanity was so thin, and I was badly shaken by this every time I visited Cathy in the lock-up ward of the hospital.

The marriage was effectively over by around 1980, although I stayed in the family home to look after Suzanne and Jonathan. This was a very difficult time for all concerned, and in the meantime, I had to earn a living. We didn't officially split up until 1985 and I had to find somewhere to stay. Clannad's Ciaran Brennan and his wife Lynda had taken a lease on The Manor, a house on Scholarstown Road in Rathfarnham. The band used to rehearse in the house, and I had a room there for a while. Sometime later I found an apartment in Sandymount, a Dublin beachside suburb. Being an early riser all my life, I enjoyed early morning walks along Sandymount strand which allowed me time to think before the day with all its distractions really began.

This was an important and traumatic period of transition for me on different fronts, moving from a family situation to living on my own and trying to plot some kind of a future. It also meant some short-term (I hoped) sacrifices. For example, long gone was the brand-new Ford Capri to be replaced by a 12-year-old Renault 4L and at one low point, I reckoned I was just about down to my last fiver.

So with little else to do I spent the first six months of 1991 in my apartment in Sandymount looking at the Gulf War on television all day every day, watching Stormin' Norman re-taking Kuwait from Iraqi leader Saddam Hussein.

When I wasn't preoccupied with the Gulf War I applied myself to building up my own music publishing catalogue and signed publishing deals with a few local acts such as Blink, Speranza, Celtic Tenors, Hazel O'Connor of *Breaking Glass* fame (ask your grandparents again) and others. However, I knew from past experiences, especially the Clannad days, that it wasn't really possible to earn a living from publishing in a domestic market like Ireland alone. You had to have an international dimension to the business.

I briefly toyed with the idea of moving to Nashville to base my business there, attracted by the fact that Nashville is the home of one of my favourite music genres, country music. With hindsight, that old 20/20 vision, I'm glad I didn't follow through on that because the publishing business requires a level of objectivity that can fly out the window and you then risk signing songs and songwriters because you like them, and not because it's the right business decision. Of course, it can happen that signing a song you really like might inspire you to try harder, but it can just as easily be a distraction.

That dilemma, of the heart ruling the head, is a dangerous temptation in all areas of the music business, and you have to bring a cooler approach to decision-making, especially those that can cost you money. Sure, when you become as rich as Richard Branson you can casually indulge your personal whims but establishing a music publishing company from zero and on one shoestring doesn't allow much room for indulgence.

My Irish-based music publishing companies, Foxrock Music & Covert Music Productions were affiliated to the UK-run PRS (Performing Rights Society) who collected money in Ireland and Britain for the public use of copyright music. They collected from RTE, for example, and were expected to pay the appropriate amounts to the copyright owners. I really didn't rate their performance if you'll excuse the pun, and I felt it was long overdue to have an Irish owned collection agency.

Although the PRS had a Dublin office managed by Pat Condron and staffed by two people, it was effectively governed by the PRS in London. It seemed extraordinary to me and other music industry observers in Ireland that the PRS was overseeing the entire country with such a tiny staff. As somebody at the time said, the Dublin office was like one of the last fuckin' outposts of the British Empire!

But the natives had had enough of it and were getting very restless. Irish publishers like me were fomenting a revolt and seeking independence from their colonial masters. But, not to our surprise, PRS dismissed our initial overtures regarding independence. Their high-handedness only fuelled the resolve of Irish songwriters and publishers, and we were clearly heading into a long, hard battle.

Irish music industry professional publishers such as myself, Peter Bardon, Michael O'Riordan and top songwriters like Brendan Graham and Jimmy MacCarthy were all keen to see a collection agency in Ireland that was more intrinsically Irish than PRS could ever be. The Brits never really understood that the Irish were a completely different cultural breed unto themselves...

they still don't really. The relationship with the other collection agency, MCPS (Mechanical Copyright Collection Society), was much more positive and wasn't a contentious issue.

As a response to continuing PRS intransigence, in 1983 Irish writers and publishers set up the Irish Advisory Committee (IAC) whose role was to advise PRS in London about writing and publishing matters pertaining to Ireland. I was a founder member of the IAC and was appointed deputy chairman, and the battle for Irish independence commenced with our UK counterparts. After years of wrangling and arguing our case, they finally relented and in 1988 IMRO (Irish Music Rights Organisation) was formed as a subsidiary of PRS. Again, I was one of the founder Directors. At one meeting Brendan Graham, Chairman (who later became one of our most successful songwriters with classic songs like, 'You Raise Me Up'), went around the table and asked individual songwriters and publishers present as to what they wanted, and every one of us said, independence, and that's when the real push began.

We strongly felt the need to show the PRS how inefficiently they were doing their job in Ireland as that would build our case for complete independence. It was clear (to us Paddies) that under PRS's feeble operation there were hundreds of locations in Ireland using music without a public performance licence. By law, any commercial premises using music must have such a license.

So in 1991 I was appointed as IMRO's Infringement Officer, although people in the industry used to refer to me as 'The Music Police', and my role for about the next three years was to visit a city or town in rural Ireland and spend a weekend checking out the various establishments refusing to pay for the use of copyright music, including shops, bars, supermarkets, hairdressing salons, sunbed studios, aerobics classes, dentists' waiting-rooms and so on. I'd call into a list of pubs, hotels, discos, cafes and such places, privately noting the copyright music being played, as well as the time and date for use as evidence in the event of a later court case.

We were constantly coming up against pub and hotel owners claiming they only played traditional music that was out of copyright, or that they only put the radio or television on for the news, or whatever excuse they could invent in order not to pay. As far as I and my colleagues were concerned, they were stealing money from songwriters and publishers, including Irish songwriters who might have no other means of income, so we had little patience for petty excuses.

Those infringement visits often threw up some interesting and, looking back, some hilarious challenges for me as an undercover music police officer. For example, on a visit to Limerick City, my list included a bridal wear shop reported to be playing music without a licence from IMRO. It struck me immediately that a man in a bridal store, browsing wedding dresses, might seem rather odd, so after giving it some thought I concocted a cunning plan. I rushed in through the door and, looking frantically around the shop, breathlessly said to one of the assistants, 'Excuse me, did you see my fiancée, I'm supposed to meet her here. Has she arrived? She's got black hair and she's average height. I'm running late! She'll fuckin' kill me'. The assistant assured me there was nobody on the premises answering that description, so feigning relief I asked if I could wait. They told me that was fine, so I sat in a chair for about 20 minutes, making mental notes of the music playing in the background. When I thought I'd gathered enough evidence, I invented some excuse and left. As they say, 'necessity is the mother of invention'!

Another time I was sitting at the bar in a guest house in Waterford City when somehow the conversation came around to IMRO and the owner started pontificating about royalties and collection agencies and so on, before blurting out, 'As for those fuckers in IMRO, I don't think they exist at all.' I turned to him and said, 'Don't they?' I deliberately placed my IMRO ID card in front of him on the bar and said, 'Eh, yeah, we do!' I might've been undercover, but I was a fucker with a badge!

One infringement trip I remember well was around 1995 when Hugh Duffy, then the CEO of IMRO and one of the driving forces towards IMRO independence, advised me of two premises near the border with Northern Ireland who weren't paying their IMRO bills. In fact, the owner of one demanded to see someone from IMRO as he wasn't at all happy to have received a bill from us, and Hugh asked if I'd call in, identify myself, and speak to him. When I arrived I found a large extremely well-stocked store with goods probably worth millions. After I introduced myself he produced an IMRO bill for €150 for his annual license, which he described as outrageous.

So I said, 'What's your problem?'

He roared back at me, '€150 quid a year just to play music?'

I said, 'I have a simple solution, turn the music off and you'll have no bill'.

'But then the store would have no atmosphere!' he exclaimed.

So I pointed to his window display and said, 'You use an attractive window display to bring people into your shop, just like you use the atmosphere you say music creates to impress your customers. You pay somebody to install your window display, so in the same way, you have to pay for the music you use as well.'

He had no answer to that and paid up.

Another outlet in the same town wasn't so civilised. Remember, this was the time of the troubles in Northern Ireland and this was also a large border town I was in. I went to visit a pub which I initially found hard to locate and had to ask for directions. The reason I hadn't been able to find it was because it had no identifying sign outside.

At that time my new girlfriend (of two weeks) Colette was with me, and we tentatively entered the venue. The first thing that struck me was the pub was quite noisy with talk, but the second we walked in, a deathly hush came upon the place and virtually every pair of eyes turned to look at us. That's not totally unheard of in Ireland, but then I noticed the music playing was one of the more aggressive rebel ballads by The Wolfe Tones, and I instinctively felt very uneasy. This place seemed like it could be a hub for Republican activity. I realised we could've easily stumbled into a nest of murderers, terrorists, thieves, torturers and bank robbers!

We ordered a (very short) drink and downed it quickly, all the while looking intently at a local newspaper's crossword. Then, I told Colette to go to the Ladies and when she got out, to leave and get back to the car as quickly as possible. When I went into the Gents myself, a guy came into the urinal beside me. He didn't say anything, but it was as if he was making it clear I was unwelcome. So I got the fuck outta there as quickly as I could myself.

The following morning I went to the local Garda station and explained what I was trying to do on behalf of IMRO.

The cop advised me not to go there as it was a regular hang-out for Provisional IRA men and I just might not come out in one piece.

I relayed his advice to Colette and we left town in a hurry. In fact, I experienced similar feelings of being in bandit territory while visiting other pubs close to the border. It's interesting to note while some of these people were prepared to kill or be killed for Ireland, they had no qualms about stealing money from the very Irish songwriters they loved to listen to.

We met with a similar attitude from some discos who didn't want to pay for the music they used. As I would say to them, 'Why don't you try to run your disco with no music?' Such venues don't expect to use electricity without paying for it, so why should they assume that music should be free for them to make money from? In practical terms, music is one of the key ingredients they use to generate income, and it's no more logical to suggest they shouldn't have to pay for it than to claim they shouldn't have to pay for the wine, the drinks, or food they serve. Unfortunately, the PRS was so ineffective in Ireland that numerous people never considered the idea that any music they used had to be paid for. In time, and with a lot of energy, patience and effort, we (IMRO) were able to change those attitudes.

Slowly but surely the battle for independence was being won and in 1996 IMRO gained complete independence from PRS and started to operate as a stand-alone collection agency in Ireland, linked into the global collection network which includes PRS in the UK, GEMA in Germany and so on. Hugh Duffy often said that under the old PRS regime, Ireland had been like a giant supermarket that people could pilfer from at will, but IMRO came in and erected check-outs. Initially, people saw this as just another tax. But in due course, they became sufficiently educated and accepted that copyright music has to be paid for, just like electricity and television licenses and refuse removal services. I think the penny really dropped when IMRO started taking people to court and winning cases, leaving venue owners not only paying for their IMRO license but substantial legal bills as well.

Some argued they were only using traditional music which they felt should be free of copyright. IMRO had already acknowledged it wouldn't be charging for live, impromptu sessions of genuine traditional music where the publicans weren't charging a public admission fee. But when we checked we'd find their notion of traditional Irish music included modern compositions like, 'The Fields of Athenry' written by Pete St John in the 1970s, or 'Song For Ireland', which isn't even an Irish composition at all, having been written by the English couple Phil and June Colclough in the latter half of the last century.

We also met some resistance from musicians who claimed that what IMRO was doing was affecting their gig prospects and therefore, their income. They failed to realise that by allowing people to avoid paying for copyright music that it would be even more likely to affect their earning potential and that of other Irish songwriters and composers.

One of the court cases that became a significant turning point in favour of IMRO occurred when the Vintners Federation of Ireland (a trade body of publicans) used the Tatler Jack pub in the tourist town of Killarney in County Kerry as the basis on which to fight a test case against IMRO. I'd visited the pub several times gathering infringement evidence as to the copyright music they were using in the pub. It's always puzzled me as to why they picked that particular pub since it had a widespread reputation locally as a good music venue, but here they were trying to argue (in court) that the music played in the pub 'just happened' with no organisational input from the pub itself, although even that would probably not have won the argument.

Their defence fell apart in court when it was pointed out that their live music events were advertised in advance nearly every week in *The Kerryman* newspaper mentioning the names of artists due to play. They attempted to explain this away on the basis that somebody else was placing the ads. They used the same argument to explain how sandwich boards appeared outside on the pavement promoting that evening's musical entertainment. I know the people in Kerry are very generous, but I've never met one of them so generous as to pay for newspaper ads and organise on-site advertisements for an establishment they had no connection to. It was one of the most bizarre and funniest court cases I ever attended.

From that point on there was a general acceptance by publicans that music had to be paid for, and IMRO in time reached an amicable agreement with the VFI over copyright music licensing. As music publishing in Ireland thrived, I was invited to serve as a member of the Irish Music Copyright Reform Group (IMCRG) and was a founder member of the IBEC Music Industry Group, and Secretary of the Music Publishers Association of Ireland (MPAI). Towards the end of 1993 I'd persuaded the promoter, Denis Desmond that I could run his publishing arm The Evolving Music Company, and that, added to my IMRO work and my *Covert* operations, meant I had a decent income again. I took considerable satisfaction from seeing IMRO going from strength to strength and being such an invaluable port-of-call for Irish songwriters in need of advice and information.

Of course, IMRO also collects money on behalf of international music publishers and songwriters which is paid to the copyright owners through the global network that IMRO links into. Those global collection agencies differ in both size and levels of efficiency from country to country. The IMRO board of today consists of up to 15 individuals, a mix of songwriters and music publishers, including a Chairman and up to three external directors who are neither songwriters nor publishers but are chosen by the Board for their expertise in other relevant areas. That mix provides a very positive array of perspectives and is most illuminating, with some bringing a primarily creative viewpoint and others having a more business-oriented focus. By comparison, its Italian equivalent has over 60 board members, including three representatives of the government, which must be fun when the time comes for decision making.

It's also important to get the balance right between expenditure and income. I know of one national agency in Eastern Europe that has a string of offices around the country, but the costs of running and staffing those offices eats substantially into the money to be distributed to the legitimate copyright owners. So I'm proud and delighted to have served on the boards of both IMRO and MPCS (Ireland) and to have played a part in making IMRO once of the most respected and efficient collection agencies in the world. To have done so alongside such stalwart performers as Christy Moore, Paul Brady,

Eleanor McEvoy, Liam O Maonlai, Steve Wall, Brendan Graham and fellow publishers like Michael O'Riordan, Peter Bardon and several others, has been an added pleasure and a tremendous learning experience.

Chapter Eight

THE INTERNATIONAL DIMENSION

Prior to the arrival of the Internet, one of the most valuable opportunities for interacting with the international music industry was to visit the annual MIDEM event originally held every January in Cannes, in the South of France. MIDEM is the music industry equivalent of the Cannes Film Festival. In fact, Cannes has become a major convention town, with something like 150 annual conventions taking place there. One week you could have MAPIC, for the international property market, and another week it hosts ILTM for the luxury travel industry, and so on. Only a small number of them focus on the entertainment media, including MIP TV and MIPCOM (both of those deal with the TV market), the famous Cannes Film Festival, and MIDEM.

MIDEM is short for the Marché International du Disque et de l'Edition Musicale, and it describes itself as the annual music exhibition, conference, festival, showcase and meeting point for the global music industry. The hub of the event is in the Palais des Festivals on the Promenade de la Croissette, a purpose-built six-storey convention centre erected in 1979 to replace the previous building which became unsuitable. Ironically, given the risky nature of the music industry, the new site was previously the location of a casino.

The first MIDEM took place in 1967, and I've attended almost every year since my first visit in 1979 when I was representing Scoff, although in later years I was there with my Clannad, IMRO, Celtic Woman, Covert, and

Evolving hats on. My first visit was quite an overwhelming eye-opener, 15,000 delegates drawn from the world of music, and all there to do business. In another way, it was quite consoling to discover there were thousands of like-minded industry types in the same situation as I was in, working with small labels in Germany, Canada and elsewhere, and all facing the same challenges as I was facing. I estimated that about two-thirds of the delegates were already reasonably established in the industry, while the rest were struggling, like me, to get a toe-hold.

From the beginning it was a hugely educational experience, meeting and listening to the world's top practitioners in the field of the music business in general and music publishing in particular and I haven't stopped learning since. I observed first-hand how the music publishing industry worked at the highest international level and saw how a song might be ideal for certain markets but didn't have the same potential for others. I learned that while you can never overlook local factors, you also have to focus on the big picture and a minor hit in a large market can generate more money than a major number one in a small market.

I've also found the seminars, workshops and conferences extremely informative. I especially recall attending conferences in the late 1990s and early 2000s when the Internet was first beginning to make its mark. They featured expert speakers like Gerd Leonhard, who have the ability to foresee how new trends and developments can impact your business. I vividly recall one speaker making a very prophetic announcement about the impending impact of the Internet when he said, 'The bath is full to the brim with water and duckies, and the big guy is about to get in!'

The speakers were often right there at the cutting edge of what was happening that we didn't know about but would soon be upon us. Some experts are very smart at being able to see how totally new developments will impinge on the industry years down the line. From them, we first heard about concepts like downloads, iTunes, streaming and so on. Back when they first spoke about the information super-highway, it was a totally unknown concept to the vast majority of people. But now we travel on it every day!

It didn't take me long to develop my bullshit-detecting-antenna, as you can waste serious amounts of your time being collared by loudmouths who want to do nothing more than tell you how important they are, the celebrities and high-flyers they know, how much they made out of this or that deal, and all sorts of other rubbish. They waste time that's costing you money and drain your energy and patience. So after a while you instinctively recognise these guys before they get too close, so you can take swift evasive action.

Many musicians and bands over the years have asked me if I think they should go to MIDEM. I point out that it's going to cost them at least a couple of thousand euros. So unless they have something that's so strong it's going to catch the attention of their target market, they might be better spending that money on something that'll bring a more obvious benefit. The music industry is extremely competitive, and that level of competition is very much in evidence at MIDEM. So any illusions anyone might have that MIDEM is a playground or a casual holiday should be left at the airport. It's way too expensive for that. Anyone can attend if they wish, providing they pay the enrolment cost of about €800, so it really only attracts those with a serious interest in doing business. On arrival, you check-in and are given your badge for the week. That badge will gain you access to most key events you want to attend and most of the areas you need to visit, such as the Palais itself, including all the exhibition stands and even some of the hotels. But you must make sure not to lose your badge, as it now costs €1,200 to replace.

You collect a copy of the MIDEM guide which is a mammoth publication only available to delegates. It's an invaluable item for making contacts, as it lists information for all the delegates and the companies represented. Naive newbies comb through this and think, 'Oh, great. I see Doug Morris, the Chairman and CEO of SONY Music Entertainment, is here. I'll want to meet him and play him a demo of my new act, so I'll drop by the Sony stand tomorrow.' But that's not going to happen. Most of the top guys such as Morris don't hang around their own stands but have a pre-arranged schedule of appointments made long before they left the USA, and they're more likely to take place in private hotel suites. The sixth floor of the convention centre is usually reserved for the elite, and even your official badge doesn't gain you entrance without an appointment. So my advice for newbies is to do as much research in advance rather than waiting until you arrive, as by then the most sought-after delegates will have filled their diaries.

On one of my early visits to MIDEM, I vowed that one day I'd get to the sixth floor, and this indeed happened with the success of Celtic Woman and the people from Fujipacific, an enormous entertainment corporation from Japan invited me to meet them on the sixth floor to discuss a sub-publishing deal. In fact, they actually flew Johnny Fingers in specifically to ensure I was on the level. I'd known Johnny from the Boomtown Rats days. He'd lived in Dun Laoghaire not far from me, and he was by now working as a consultant in Japan. There was a lot at stake and I don't blame Fuji for being cautious.

Alongside the cost of enrolling for MIDEM, Cannes is an expensive place to stay, and apart from those who are on expenses from their corporations, most delegates are under pressure to earn back their investment in time and money. The top-line hotels like The Carlton, The Majestic and The Martinez, are all located around the famous Croisette beachfront, and you have to book them through the MIDEM organisation who take a percentage commission, as they do from taxi drivers, restaurants and just about everything else. You could opt to stay in a hotel out of town, but then you have to allow for the cost and inconvenience of travelling in and out maybe several times each day.

I arrived in Cannes a few days early one year and saw the waiters remove their menus and replace them with the much more expensive MIDEM menus. To give you some example of the cost of eating, I wouldn't be surprised to be charged €25 for a basic omelette and chips at a beachfront restaurant. But up near the railway station, maybe 4/5 streets away, you could have the same meal for about €5. But, of course, the top cats are more likely to be on the Croisette, so if you're chasing them, you won't find them in the €5 omelette spots.

Drinks are equally expensive. A couple of years ago I ordered a small bottle of Kronenbourg 1664 beer in the bar of the Carlton Hotel. It duly arrived with a bill for €12.50. I was staying in a self-contained apartment and earlier that day I'd bought a six-pack of the same beer for €4.50! When the grumpy French waiter presented me with the bill I said, 'At least Dick Turpin wore a mask!', but I think that remark was lost in translation.

That reminds me of one Irish delegate who was on his first visit to MIDEM. He spotted a bunch of us sitting in the Martinez Bar. He was obviously totally unaware of the cost of drinks in the top hotels. When the drinks round we'd just ordered arrived, he shouted, 'I'll get that!' The bill used up virtually all his expense allowance for the week! Welcome to Cannes I thought...

Drinking and partying too late into the night can have another cost in that you might not make it to the first couple of your appointments the following morning, so your reputation for being unreliable will start to travel around ahead of you. You really need to stay focused on the business at hand and exercise great discipline. You might think you can concentrate on the business during the day and treat the evenings as if you were on holiday, but that can be a hard plan to stick to. I've always lived by the 'work hard, play hard' ethos. The music business is no place for semi-professional attitudes and in fact, it's generally run by people who turn up when and where they're expected.

Some companies have lavish stands in the main display areas, while others hustle optimistically on their own. For some people it must be overwhelming, caught in the middle of a mad whirl where artists are being signed or turned down, record distribution deals are contracted, tours are set up and music publishing or sub-publishing arrangements negotiated, among numerous other industry-related activities. You might, for example, after successful negotiations, arrange for your record label to have distribution in Japan, or link an artist you manage with a tour promoter in Canada with a view to organising a nationwide tour there. A showcase gig for an artist might excite interest in record companies, publishing companies or tour promoters in one or more territories. It's quite conceivable that a successful visit to MIDEM might transform the status of an artist from a minor figure to a major player. Or, in my own case, I might conclude a deal for a publishing company in Australia to handle some, or all, of my catalogue there.

In essence, MIDEM is only as good as you make it. If you go there naively expecting things to happen automatically you'll be very disappointed, and you'll be a few grand down. Attending MIDEM can be something of an endurance test. On a typical day you might have two or three meetings each morning and afternoon, followed by a business dinner at 8pm, then a late-night visit to a bar, perhaps to follow up on some contacts made earlier. So you might get to bed at 3am and have to do it all over again the next day. As you can imagine, it requires a lot of walking, a lot of talking and a lot of bullshit.

I'd make it my business to drop by several times a day to the Irish stands to check the list of visitors to the stand and see who might've been looking for me. Often the list would be too long to get back to them all, and I'd have to assess the likely return on responding to this or that request for a meeting or a listening session. You might imagine that MIDEM is very noisy, with music blaring out of an endless line of speakers at stands and along the streets, but not so. You can walk along the Croissette, which is about half a mile long, and see people listening to music on their personal stereos or iPods. Or you might bump into Paul McGuinness who, even when he was the manager of U2 when they were the biggest band in the world (still are in my view), is generally very approachable and willing to give time to people who might need advice or information. Indeed, subject to the normal constraints of time and other commitments, the top people in the music industry are often surprisingly accessible and approachable.

You can also learn much by simply observing the inventiveness of others. When YouTube started to attend the convention they organised a representative for virtually every key national stand. This was a terrific way of building their profile in each country, sending out a message to the worldwide industry that they were serious about their commitment to music. It also proves how important a presence at MIDEM was for them.

There are countless live showcase gigs in places like the Irish bar Morrison's on Rue Teisseire, a couple of streets away from the main drag. Acts of the calibre of Lionel Richie, Boney M, Diana Ross, Pete Townshend, David Gilmour, Stevie Wonder, Phil Collins and Amy Winehouse have played live in various venues at MIDEM. So have thousands of emerging acts who might at the time be established in their home countries but are now hoping to make a break onto the international stage, including a strong annual Irish presence.

Regular Irish attendees included independent record labels like Reekus Records, Round Tower, Dolphin, Claddagh, Danceline, Crashed Records, K-tel and others. Publishers such as Michael O'Riordan, Peter Bardon and Shay Hennessy were also regulars, as well as organisations of the stature of IMRO. The Northern Ireland industry would also have a presence, including Emerald Records and Sharp Records. Smaller companies would arrange to be represented by somebody like myself if they couldn't afford to have their own representation.

While IMRO have always been consistently supportive of the Irish presence at MIDEM, I've always been disappointed, and have said as much, by the lack of interest of the IFPI, (Irish Federation of Phonographic Industry) the organisation who represent the major and (to a lesser extent) independent record companies in Ireland. Given how well most of them have done over the decades from the Irish market, it wouldn't be out of place if they were to show even a token of support for the home industry, but virtually all of them are governed by their Masters in London who see no commercial benefit in their doing so. So it's very rare to see any representatives from the Irish majors or, indeed, from any other industry body apart from IMRO. National broadcasters too have been spectacularly indifferent to what is effectively an international showcase event for one of Ireland's most high-profile industries.

There was a great flurry of excitement one year about the UK ska band Bad Manners who are just one of the countless acts to be signed at MIDEM. Their frontman, Buster Bloodvessel, was a larger-than-life character and he strutted around Cannes in a day-glow suit that was hard to ignore. Other tricks used to attract attention to specific acts could include the use of scantily-clad ladies handing out leaflets for showcase gigs. People dress in all kinds of strange costumes that sometimes turn Cannes into a bit of a circus.

There was considerable excitement in 1994 when the Irish promoter Robert Stephenson organised a MIDEM Irish showcase which featured Paddy Casey, Damien Dempsey and Dr Millar. It was attended by our now President Michael D Higgins, then our Minister for Arts, Culture and the Gaeltacht and one of the few government ministers who has an understanding of the value of the Irish music and the industry. Other Irish acts showcased at MIDEM over the years include Joe Dolan and Paddy Moloney (Chieftains).

Not that this always works out smoothly either. When I arrived at Nice airport on my way to MIDEM one year, I bumped into the manager of an up-and-coming Irish music star. It was the manager's first visit to MIDEM, so I asked him what was he there for. He proudly told me that his artist was playing live at MIDEM. I expressed some surprise at this as I hadn't seen this artist's name in the events listing, so I asked where his act was performing. 'He's playing at a venue called Juan-Les-Pin.' I didn't have the heart to tell him that Juan-Les-Pin is not a venue but a different town about 9 kilometres away from Cannes.

The music on offer each year extends across all genres, from classical music to rock, jazz, blues, pop, urban, dance rap and reggae to all types of world music. On Saturday nights there's the presentation of the French music Television Awards which is a serious and very exclusive red-carpet event that attracts massive public and industry interest.

Every year there's a focus on a specific country who host the opening night gala, with a lavish reception followed by special live performances by top and up-and-coming acts from that country on several stages, alongside samples of their cuisine and other aspects of their culture. Elsewhere, around Cannes, you might have off-shoot showcase gigs featuring more talent from that country. This costs a packet, anywhere from half a million up, so Ireland has never been able to afford to host such a night. Having said that, we're now such a key player in the music world, an Irish delegate can be a serious target for all kinds of people wanting to give you material in the hopes you can help them break into our market. It takes all your diplomatic skills to tell the aggressive representative of, say, a Hungarian folk troupe, there's not much of a market in Ireland for what they have to offer. You also have to keep your eyes wide open for scams. One year I noticed a number of cars parked along some of the streets with what I presumed were hookers looking for business. But, I was told later they were actually transvestites. I know of one Irish delegate who also thought they were female and found out the hard way that they weren't. I suspect that came as a bit of a shock to him!

Another trick they try on those who might be in the company of an attractive lady but are running low on cash. She'll try to persuade you to get some more money from a nearby ATM so you can continue to entertain her because she loves your company so much. But, she has accomplices waiting so as soon as you get the cash they take it off you and all disappear. But, that happens everywhere.

Nor does one's MIDEM work end when you check out of the hotel to fly home. Back in the days when CDs and cassette tapes, (another one for your grandfather!) were the methods of consuming music, I'd often arrive back home with an extra suitcase full of records, brochures, magazines, documents, business cards, my own notes and observations, and all sorts of other paraphernalia, most of which has to be carefully evaluated and followed up as appropriate.

Ironically, the arrival of the Internet, which I first really learned about at MIDEM, has lessened the intensity of MIDEM which initially grew from the convenience of being able to meet people you needed to meet, but all in one place and in one week. Back then there was nothing like it and no other way, and serious players in the industry would plan their calendar around MIDEM. There are no borders with the Internet, no travel costs and no need to book hotels. When I first started doing business with international contacts we had an appalling phone system in Ireland. Now we can talk to each other on a daily basis via Skype, phones, e-mails and probably several other means they haven't told us about! Whereas at one time you had to have demos to hand around to all delegates you thought might be interested in your song or act, now you can create a website, upload as many tracks as you like, have your own YouTube channel, send a Soundcloud link via Twitter, Snapchat or Instagram and interested parties can access it any time they like all year round.

I lament that in a way, but it's all part of the ever-changing industry in which I've opted to make my career. I still believe the face-to-face encounter is just as important now because the music industry is a people business. People prefer to work with those they know and trust, and it's hard to develop those relationships at arm's length. When you meet somebody, maybe have a meal together, or enjoy a drink and a chat, you can get a clearer sense of whether you might be able to work with that person or not. A more relaxed situation allows people to sit back and express views and ambitions that can be quite casual but can often lead to a meeting of minds and the generation of creative ideas that wouldn't happen as easily without the personal get-together. And that's why MIDEM came into existence in the first place.

That said the numbers who attend today are substantially down from the 15,000 since the days when I first attended. While it always took place in the early part of the year, in 2014 they moved it to June and the attendance was probably around 5,000. A friend from South Africa told me that in 2015 he'd been to MIPCOM (Marché International des Programmes de Communication or International Market of Communications Programmes) and there were 15,000 at that festival. But there was a time when those numbers would've been reversed. Companies and organisations that perhaps used to send 12 delegates to MIDEM now might send 3. But the 3 they do send will be the key-players from the company, and therefore very worthwhile to get a meeting with.

Now there's talk that MIDEM might move to Barcelona, which would have many advantages. It might actually save it, or at least keep it alive for a few more years. Ireland would also have the facilities to host MIDEM? Indeed, some enterprising young colleagues of mine in the industry have recently started a small convention called Music Cork in Ireland's second city, which I attended in 2018 and found very worthwhile and extremely well run. They had great young speakers and a very attentive audience. Cannes was no fun in minus 4 degrees, and you're walking half a mile in the rain, so you won't hear me complain if it moves to Spain. Then again, there are some who predict the Internet will eventually kill MIDEM.

Attending MIDEM has brought me much satisfaction in seeing first-hand, how Ireland's role in the global music market has developed from being small-fry to the point where we're now regarded as big players and so many people want to do business with us. It's changed in another, more personal way too, in the strange way that the music world sometimes works.

On my first visit way back in 1979 I was the newbie trying to persuade key industry figures to give me the time of day, that situation has now come full circle, and following the international success of my clients such as Celtic Woman and Hozier, I feel like I'm among the echelon of those who are being sought after. From the hustler to the hustled... I have to admit that's a pleasant feeling.

Chapter Nine

GOVERNMENTS AND MUSIC

In the previous chapter, I referred to how a country would host a special night during MIDEM in order to showcase the music and other attractions of that country. I imagine such a display must have a positive impact on the country's tourism industry too. So it seems strange to me, especially given how important both music and tourism are to Ireland, that we've never had a focus on Ireland at MIDEM in all the decades the event has been running, and despite the increasing profile Irish music has earned within the international music community.

In 2017 IMRO commissioned *Deloitte* to produce a report called *The Socio-Economic Contribution of Music to the Irish Economy*. It argued that music contributes more than €700 million annually to the Irish economy and that employment in the music industry stands at over 13,000. As revered an international figure as Robbie Williams told the producers of the report that, 'Playing in Ireland is always one of the highlights of my tours. I always look forward to coming to Ireland, the crowd is always amazing and there seems to be an incredible connection between audience and performer. Ireland has a special place in its heart for live music.'

Indeed, it's been well documented how the success of U2, *Riverdance* and numerous other acts have attracted many people to Ireland, and how important music is to visitors, not just performers like Williams, but music fans who flock here every year. Paul McGuinness, when he was manager of

U2, always registered his company Principle Management at the Irish stand. That alone was an enormous boost to this country. Yet I've never really felt that any Irish government has given the Irish music industry the support it deserves.

The Irish stand at MIDEM probably costs about €75,000, and our government makes a minor contribution to that, but it's small beer compared to the kind of support other governments, including Cuba and Finland, have contributed to their music industry's presence at MIDEM. Paltry government interest in the Irish music industry might result from a lack of understanding as to how it works, or because they don't see votes in it. I've always assumed it's the latter because I regard everything that politicians do and say as having only one purpose, to get them elected or re-elected. Yes, musicians can be useful for photo opportunities, but that's as far as it goes with most politicians. Yet, despite their indifference, Ireland punches well above its weight on the international music market.

It used to amuse many of us when representatives from what was *An Bord Trachtala* (the Irish Export Board) would arrive at the Irish stand trying to look important. I saw no value in their attendance and I never saw them doing anything of any substance. I remember one particular year looking at their head honcho lurking around the Irish stand looking about as useful as a chocolate teapot. I think his name was Charlie (something). I said, 'Charlie, come with me'. I brought him into the middle of the exhibition space, over to a huge big gleaming stand that looked so cool, well-lit and decorated and I asked him, 'Do you know which country this stand represents?' He looked nonplussed and answered, 'No' I said. 'This is the Swiss stand. Do you know the last successful music that came out of Switzerland?' Before he could answer I said, 'The fuckin' cuckoo clock!' (Yes, I know, but before you call Joe Duffy I know the Swiss didn't invent the cuckoo clock. But it's one of those clichés that has been repeated so often it's nearly true). It annoyed me that the Swiss could have such a spectacular presence when Ireland, the fifth largest provider of talent to the world market, had to deal with far more enquiries at a stand that was a mere 40 feet square and stuck in a corner.

On my return from Cannes, I received questionnaires from the Irish

Export people asking me, among other questions, 'How many records did you sell there?' They seem to put no value on the contacts you make, on the basis of which much later business can be conducted, or that a manager might have a hugely successful MIDEM at which he signed several deals for his artist that might not bear fruit for a couple of years. I suspect it's partly due to a lack of imagination and knowledge and they need to justify their large salaries by wanting to see actual sales of actual records as if MIDEM were some kind of international car boot sale.

I appreciate the government's attention is focused more sharply on the major corporations who can bring more jobs to Ireland and besides whom the Irish music industry might appear to be less important in short-term economics. But, if that's how they see us, why don't they have the honesty to admit that? Besides, the Irish music scene has more to offer Irish society than economic benefits anyway, even if those benefits are in terms of education, self-expression, culture and tourism. Of course, there's also the issue of the industry's lack of lobbying power. There are so many other sectors who seem to have this down to a fine art and who can wangle one concession after another from any government ministry they choose to target. And what chance has the music industry anyway when it's up against corporations as globally powerful as Google, Facebook, Apple and the rest of the tech giants?

Of course, the music industry's relationship with the government is not helped by the inevitable changes of government, and/or the minister with responsibility for the arts and culture under which music tends to fall. You can spend years building up a relationship with one government or one particular minister only to have to start all over again after the next election or after a routine spot of musical chairs in the cabinet room.

When Michael D Higgins was Minister for The Arts, Culture and The Gaeltacht we at least had a man who saw the value in all arts and culture and was a big music fan. Then along came an election after which we had a change of government and John O'Donoghue was appointed minister for Arts, Sport and Tourism. One might have imagined any one of these three areas would be sufficient for one man, but not the Boul' O'Donoghue. The fact that music would be lumped in somewhere with two other major subjects says it all really.

Recent photo taken with an old friend. A great Statesman.
The world needs more men like President Michael D Higgins

Michael D set up the Task Force on the Music Industry and when its report came out in 1996 one of its main recommendations was the introduction of a Music Board comparable to The Irish Film Board. This made perfect sense, especially as Michael D said that whenever he needed to talk to the Irish music industry he didn't know where to start because it was fragmented into so many sections and sub-sections.

The next government eventually agreed to introduce The Irish Music Board but supported with a derisory contribution and a set-up which seemed to be geared almost exclusively towards the Irish traditional and country music sectors. Maybe that's where the votes are. But there was nobody on the board who was seen as having a specific expertise in the rock end of the industry, an inexplicable move given the Irish rock music sector was already accepted as a major contributor to the global music market. While some, including myself, have argued from time to time for more government involvement in, and support for, the Irish music business, there are others who'd prefer they stayed away from it altogether because they probably have nothing to contribute except interference. Perhaps, The Irish Music Board debacle supports that argument? Personally, given the amount of our money that governments can squander in all sorts of other areas, (such as storing expensive and redundant electronic voting machines) I want to encourage them to give the Music Industry the support it deserves. After all, why should we be ignored? Unfortunately, we've never been able to get an Irish government to commit to anything meaningful in support of the Irish music industry. But, I live in hope.

It was with much of that in mind that IMRO commissioned *The Socio-Economic Contribution of Music to the Irish Economy*. It argued that there are significant opportunities to be opened up in job creation, exports, commerce and education for Ireland's indigenous music industry if the appropriate support structures are put in place. But whether our governments will ever care or not remains to be seen.

Part of the problem is that little or nothing originates with the government or its agencies. They appear to respond to what other people and organisations bring to them but have no creative input themselves. They seem to spend more time sorting out potholes and small matters that deliver votes rather than being inventive about anything as important as music in Ireland. But I believe the afore-mentioned document will have a considerable impact because of its clarity and because its arguments are supported with facts and figures. There may have been a tendency in the past to produce material that was possibly baffling to those not already familiar with the structure of the music industry in Ireland, but this one spells it out.

One of the key government-related issues that keeps cropping up is that of a quota system for Irish music on Irish radio. This is an old chestnut that won't go away. I remember back in the early eighties marching through the streets of Dublin with the showband manager Jim Hand and many musicians, protesting against the lack of radio play for Irish music on RTE. And it's still a live issue. In 2015 the renowned singer-songwriter, Johnny Duhan wrote several articles in *The Sunday Independent* arguing for more Irish music on Irish radio. It was encouraging for me to see a musician taking such a public stance because, with a small number of exceptions, musicians have tended to casually leave this kind of problem for others to sort out on their behalf.

I can say this from experience. I was an active member of the Jobs In Music committee (JIM) back in the mid-eighties, and one of our main arguments was for more Irish music on Irish radio. The committee arose out of a number of discussions when unemployment in Ireland was very high. The committee included the DJ Anne-Marie Walsh, Val James, the late Aiden Lambert, Eoin Holmes (later to stand as a Labour candidate in a general election), Jackie Hayden, promoter Dermot Flynn, and Eddie Joyce of Danceline Records. We were totally independent and had no money or support from any organisation, apart from a small number of rock bands who did live gigs to provide us with some funds to cover post and photo-copying and such like.

We'd meet weekly in Whelan's in Dublin and would issue regular press releases calling for more radio play. We'd also host public meetings in the Clarence Hotel, but sadly, few musicians attended those public meetings. On receipt of our press releases, newspaper journalists, eager to write about the issue, would call a few known musicians who'd invariably tell them they were very happy with the airplay they were getting. After a while, we decided if the musicians themselves weren't interested in seeing the big picture and supporting the campaign, why should we bother? So JIM was dissolved.

I've been equally bemused over the years by individuals offering themselves as candidates for the IMRO Board and promising to use their position to canvas for more Irish music on Irish radio. Much as I obviously sympathise with that sentiment, it's not an area IMRO can actively get involved in, simply because the organisation not only represents Irish songwriters but also collects revenue from radio play in Ireland for international writers.

What IMRO would be doing in effect would be campaigning for Irish radio stations to stop playing records by one sector of its membership in order to favour a different sector. I suspect any serious move down that road would risk the international acts currently represented by IMRO forming a breakaway organisation, and that would also certainly weaken IMRO's position.

Of course, there's another problem in defining exactly what constitutes an Irish record and what doesn't. Does it only refer to recordings made by Irish artists or songs written by Irish writers? Or to artists who are resident in Ireland for tax or other purposes? Or should there be a broader definition that includes any recording made in Ireland irrespective of the nationality of the artist? The latter notion gave rise to many a heated debate during which it was argued that an international star like Kate Bush recording in a studio in Dublin was more deserving of Irish radio support than an album by an Irish act singing songs written by American and British songwriters, produced in Denmark by a Norwegian production team with no Irish musicians involved other than the featured act? We accept Sinead O'Connor singing a song by Prince as an Irish record, but can Brian Ferry singing the old Irish folk song 'Carrickfergus' also be an Irish record? All of these examples are valid aspects of the argument, but I've yet to see a convincing definition that covers all eventualities. So that argument lives on.

2016 IMRO Radio Awards with Mick Hanley, Shay Healy & Philip Flynn

The response in radio-land to the JIM campaign was mixed, and I was surprised by how sensitive some of the radio people were to the criticism implicit in the campaign. I partly suspected that while the press is used to criticism, and newspapers and magazines regularly publish critical letters from readers, radio takes public criticism to heart and some sensitive souls resented that it could even arise in the first place.

Another flaw in the quota argument is that even if a higher percentage is agreed it may simply mean the stations play more U2, The Script, Hozier, Sinead O'Connor, Van Morrison, Imelda May and other artists who are internationally successful, and emerging artists would still be ignored. It understandably irritates many in the business that radio will ignore an Irish artist until they start gaining recognition overseas, and it's only then that Irish radio stations start featuring their recordings.

This has happened several times, most notably with the Cranberries who went almost totally unheard of on Irish radio outside the specialist rock shows until they started making waves in the USA. Suddenly, the same record that a few months previous wasn't suitable to play, was then given the all clear. Some responded very positively to the JIM campaign. Dermot Hanrahan and Dave Kelly at FM104 announced a 30% quota of Irish artists, and before long 98FM launched a show called *Totally Irish* hosted by Jim O'Neill and later on by Tom Dunne. Both moves provided serious boosts to Irish artists and proved that there were people in Irish radio who were prepared to listen. Although Tom Dunne moved on, the programme *Totally Irish* is still running. Sadly, our biggest pop station 2fm claimed at the time to be adhering to a 30% quota, but all the information they supplied listing the records actually played over several weeks showed they barely ever reached more than about 15% on any one day. Even when they upped that figure it was achieved by playing a lot of Irish artists at 2 or 3am when their listenership figures were at their lowest. It's a strange way for our national broadcaster to treat Irish musicians, although I'm glad to note that we, and they, have come a long way since then.

Sometime after the dissolution of JIM, the suggestion arose of acknowledging those in Irish radio stations who had been most supportive of emerging new talent. It was me and Jackie Hayden who came up with the basic concept, but Eddie Joyce made a serious contribution by inventing the snappy title Fairplay For Airplay. It was suggested we approach IMRO regarding sponsorship. Conscious that IMRO act as representatives of international artists as well as Irish, we broadened the remit of the project to take in those who were supportive of emerging talent in general, and not only Irish talent. As these were virtually the same people who had the breadth of vision to assume their listeners were adventurous enough to be open to new music, it made little difference in terms of who we chose as recipients.

So with the financial assistance of IMRO, we visited two radio stations every month and presented a DJ there with his or her Fairplay For Airplay award. Among the recipients were Jon Richards at Galway Bay FM, Roddy Cleere at WLR in Waterford, Alan McGuire at South East Radio in Wexford, and June Carley with Midlands 103. All of them were very supportive of new music, and some of them had done so in the face of barely concealed opposition within their own stations.

What the stations seemed to appreciate most about Fairplay For Airplay was that somebody was prepared to travel down to present the award, as there had been a tradition of a Dublin-centric industry expecting people to travel to Dublin for everything. In almost all cases, a modest reception was organised at which the recipient would receive his or her award.

Fairplay For Airplay was generally seen as a positive step, in that there was a widespread view that enough criticism had been directed at radio stations, and it was time to recognise those who were supportive of new talent. And thus, another job in music was well done.

Chapter Ten

ADVICE ON DEMAND

I t's often been said that the upper echelon of the music industry is inhabited by sharks. If there's money to be made in those shark-infested waters, the sharks are remarkably astute at spotting likely prey. They find them wherever they are, hunt them down and move in for the kill. For some of them, it seems like an addiction. No matter how many deals they've done they still need another fix, so it's essential that anyone entering their murky waters is ready and armed with all the knowledge they need in order to protect themselves and their music. And while the music industry is rightly regarded as a very competitive environment at all levels, I've generally found most people in the business to be generous with their time whenever I sought advice or information.

It was through observing the quirks and foibles, and the often downright bad career/business decisions made by some musicians, that I felt I wanted to share my modest knowledge with young musicians when requested. With that attitude, I was invited by the Rock School in Ballyfermot, Dublin to deliver my first lecture on music publishing around my 39th birthday. I remember arriving out in a suit (*for god's sake!*) and being very nervous about how my lecture would be received by a bunch of young students. But it went fine, and I even quite enjoyed the experience.

I was also conscious that when I was a mere novice in the business there was nowhere I could actually go for any kind of formal advice or information and I simply had to find it out piecemeal and through making my own mistakes. That said, I still find it hard to understand why young musicians are often so reluctant to understand that the music business is just what it says, a *BUSINESS!*

Apart from the extremely rich, or the extremely careless who prefer fantasy to reality, it's not a hobby. Companies survive because they generate sufficient income from making (mostly) wise decisions based on business practices that work in their best interests. Key decisions are rarely based on sentiment. Of course, there was a downside to my making myself so accessible. My mobile (or cell phone as the Americans quaintly call it) phone number is widely available in countless industry directories so I found myself regularly spending an hour with this solo artist or that band in a hotel bar, and being left to pay the €25 coffee bill and, thanks to the dismissive attitude of some of them, wondering if I'd not only been wasting my breath but my money as well.

So I hit on the idea in 1997 of writing and publishing, *The Need To Know Guide To Music Publishing* published by my own company, Foxrock Music Productions (see, there goes that fox again!) with distribution through Eason's chain of bookshops. So, when somebody asked if I could meet for a chat, I'd suggest they pick up a copy of my book and if there was anything in it they didn't understand, then, and only then, would I be willing to meet them. The book sold out and if I ever get the time I might even update it!

It was probably around that time when I realised that giving some young musicians free advice is often a complete waste of time, as they seemed to feel they knew as much about the business, if not more than I did. I admire their enthusiasm, drive and energy of youth, but when it descends into such naivety I give up. It's no fun trying to advise those who only want to listen when you're telling them what they want to hear.

So, by the late 80s and into the 90s, I found myself being invited to serve as a regular panellist for music industry seminars of one kind or another. Those events would have a mix of experts, individuals representing a record company, radio station, a music journalist, an artist manager, a publicist, an image designer, and venue promoter and so on.

What struck me about the other people from the industry or the music media taking part in these events was that while we often disagreed passionately and heatedly over the music, we rarely differed much on the practicalities of what musicians had to learn in order to lay the groundwork for a long-term career in music. They could be generous in recounting the mistakes they themselves had made. But we also tended instinctively to avoid telling musicians what they should do, as if there was a magic formula, but instead outlined a range of options, maybe discussed the pros and cons, and left the musician to take responsibility and make his or her own decision.

I'd already come to the conclusion that it's not so much the actual information you give young musicians that's important, but that you help to lead them towards asking themselves the right questions and discovering the answers for themselves. It didn't take me very long to realise that many artists haven't thought through what they're hoping to achieve or what they hope to gain from their music careers. I was often puzzled to note how few of them arrived at seminars or discussions with not so much as a pen and paper to take notes. There were no iPads or smartphones in those days.

They seemed to be led by a blind, and often misleading, faith that it will all work out perfectly in the end because they deserve it. If only life was like that! The seminars and my involvement in events like Demo Marathons, where a chosen number of acts were given a confidential and private hour with the panel of experts, were rewarding experiences and led to strange encounters with musicians both in Ireland and abroad.

While some took copious notes, others only seemed interested in you telling them that they were going to be rich and famous in a matter of months, and that somebody else would sort out their career issues for them. Unfortunately for them, the kind of people selected for such advisory panels were willing and able to tell them exactly how it is in the real world. Indeed, it would be true to say I learned much from the observations of other members of said panels.

But there were times when it was difficult to understand the mind-sets of some of those who sought our advice and opinions. At one seminar in Dublin, I had a guy ask how he could stop Paul McCartney from recording one of his songs. The likelihood of this eventuality ever troubling the lad was probably extremely remote and I don't know if he had some ideological objection to Paul, but the question smacked of a kind of paranoia that isn't helpful to someone who fancies forging a career in the highly competitive music business. I'm not sure if it's a kind of music snobbery, but it's not helpful on the career front.

The assumption that some acts had, was that we should be able to give them a five-step programme to guaranteed success, was so far off beam it beggared belief. Many would give the impression that now they'd written/recorded a classic of modern music, all they had to do was wait for the phone to ring and somebody to put money in their bank account, but when it didn't it was the music industry's fault, (including mine!). Had they never bothered to find out how their own musical heroes made it, how they took their music out to people and forged relationships in the business and in the media with those who were able to help them?

I met singer-songwriters whose main worry wasn't how to get gigs, or airplay or record deals or publicity, but how they could stop somebody at a gig stealing one of their songs and making a financial killing out of it.

Given my long years in music, and the fact that hundreds of thousands of new songs are written every year, the number of instances of song theft is tiny. It would be virtually impossible to get away with it, especially if the song was played in public, rehearsed with other musicians, posted on a website, recorded on a demo or sent as a Soundcloud link or an mp3 attachment with an e-mail. I feel that such illogical concerns are obstacles that simply impede an artist's progress as if the life of an artist wasn't complicated enough without inventing more problems.

Another chap in Limerick reckoned if he told radio stations that he'd be willing to allow them to play his songs free of charge he'd be more likely to get played because the stations would save money by doing so. The first problem is, it doesn't work like that. Radio stations pay a fixed fee or percentage of advertising revenue for the blanket use of copyright material, and this man's generosity wouldn't affect that in the slightest. But I recall saying to him, 'Why stop at giving your songs away free? Why not do all your gigs for free, give your recordings away free, as well as whatever merchandise you might have for sale?' It was a truly bizarre notion. And there were even more bizarre notions when the internet came along.

It was always easier to help those who were well-motivated, had the energy to put into moving forward and had a realistic grasp of the difficulties ahead, not least from the increasingly vast number of acts competing for the limited spending money available to their potential fans. It's important for emerging acts to realise that unless a sufficient number of people want to buy their downloads, CDs, t-shirts or tickets to their gigs, they're unlikely to have much of a career. Other industries call them customers, but we refer to them as fans, and their importance is the same no matter what name you give them.

We saw the requirements for success in the music industry as requiring skills that are arguably essential for real success in any other field. They have to expect and be able to deal with, the knock-backs and disappointments that are almost certain to face them, and many were quite impressive in the diligent way they were going about building a career for themselves. But, as is the nature of these things, the most memorable stories relate to those with issues of one kind or another.

I remember in particular a seven-piece band made up of students in Sligo. They swaggered into the room all dressed in cool leather jackets and typical rock star clothes and hairstyles, and I thought to myself, 'Well at least these guys look like a band'. When we asked what their biggest difficulty was they explained how they were finding it impossible to finish off some recordings as they were a couple of hundred quid short. When I suggested to them they could all work for a week, perhaps in McDonald's or indeed any place they would easily raise the necessary funding, they were completely horrified and looked at us as if we were nuts. In truth, the fact that they weren't prepared to sacrifice a week of their lives because it wouldn't be *cool,* proved to us how little commitment they actually had to their music, and we never heard of them again.

As said it wasn't uncommon for bands to arrive without a notebook between them in order to take down the names of people we might suggest who could, for example, give them airplay. If we pointed this out they were likely to look vaguely at each other as if a pen was something they once heard about but exactly weren't sure what one was. A band in Cork told us they'd cut back on gigging in their hometown of Midleton because they were afraid of being, 'over-exposed in Midleton'. It was impossible to fathom where this concept came from, but it struck us as totally daft, and we told them so. Imagine The Beatles deciding before they'd even made their first record, that they didn't want to play in Liverpool any more in case they got, 'over-exposed?'

An act in Galway wanted to know how they could make money from songwriting. I explained how the system worked and advised them to join a collection agency like IMRO. They were a bit nonplussed by this, and one of them even said, 'But how would we know how to contact IMRO?' I exasperatedly suggested they could find the IMRO address and phone number in the telephone book or the *Hot Press Yearbook* (no Google, remember?). 'But what would we do then?' one of them asked. I advised them to ask IMRO to send them an application form. When the thought of filling in an application form seemed to be beyond them, we gave up. We never heard of them again either. I wonder why?

In Carlow, we were speaking to a band when one of their key members admitted that he was actually planning to leave the band and had already done quite a lot of work on his debut solo album. This was news to the other members who were surprised and none too pleased. This was probably the only time in my life when I had a front-row seat at the real live break-up of a band. It was comical on one level, but sad as well.

On another occasion, I went on my own to a gig by a duo. They were quite good, and I thought they had something interesting that made me want to follow them up. I invited them to call to my office, and after speaking with them for a while I realised the two musicians had totally different notions as to what they were trying to achieve and the way they should progress. So I opted out of that particular pursuit. One of them went on to be moderately successful. The other one I believe is following a career in a religious order. Mind you, I hear there's good money in *THAT* business too!

It's always baffled me that band members were prepared to spend endless hours in writing, rehearsing and recording demos but rarely spent any time talking to each other about what they were actually trying to achieve. As the saying goes, 'If you don't know where you're going, any road will take you there.'

A band in Belfast did have a plan. They wanted to be a cult band with a small number of fans. We waggishly pointed out to them that they had already achieved that, but I'm not sure if they caught the irony of the situation. It's a strange attitude. I can't imagine a novelist saying that he or she only wanted to be read by a small number of readers.

Then my daughter Suzanne, who'd always been fascinated with the music industry, became a key figure in a project which Jackie Hayden and I launched, the MIX Course. In fact, it was my son, Jonathan, who came up with the snappy title which stands for Music Industry Xplained, which is exactly what it does.

She tells the story in greater detail in her own book, *Having It All*, but Suzanne observed that she was constantly bumping into young people who either wanted or needed to know more about the music industry and how it worked. So she devised an education course that would explain the workings of the music industry and the music media on a very practical level. She knew there were already several courses in existence around the country that taught people about music theory, performance, recording and production, but nothing that focused specifically on explaining the business side of it.

So she, Jackie and I worked out a format that included 12 weekly lectures, lecture topics and the lecturers, a media plan, an exam, a prospectus, a venue and a budget. With a determination and persistence that I suspect she might've picked up from her old man, she even persuaded U2's Dublin office to put news of the MIX Course on the U2 website.

40 students signed up for the course when it ran in The Dun Laoghaire College of Further Education. Lecturers, as well as Jackie and myself, included Steve Averil, the man who gave U2 their name, Willie O'Reilly, then head of Today FM, and Alan McEvoy who'd handled the business affairs for various Irish acts, including The Cranberries. Record producer Pete Holidai, John Carroll, manager of A House and singer-songwriter Eleanor McEvoy all offered advice from different perspectives about the art of making records and dealing with record companies alongside other speakers who were happy to give their time to help young people advance their careers.

They were invariably prepared to be honest about their own mistakes; a factor I know was much appreciated by the students. We sought lecturers' who'd tell it like it is, warts and all (especially the warts), and we avoided lecturers' who'd see the occasion as an opportunity to do a bit of grandstanding and boast about their own achievements. We were conscious that there are many in the business glad to receive help and advice from others but less enthusiastic in giving that help back, and we studiously avoided having them as part of our lecture team. We chose people who were easy to work with and highly reliable. In fact, during all the years the course ran there wasn't one single instance of a lecturer not turning up, an occupational hazard given the unpredictable nature of the business where, as I know only too well myself, you can be called at anytime to a meeting you can't avoid.

We were also of a mind that such an open-handed detailing of the realities of working in the industry might actually lead to some students realising that maybe such a career wasn't for them, and that was a useful service too, preventing people from squandering years floundering to get into an industry they mightn't be suited for. I remember Alan McEvoy making an interesting point. He said having to explain why we do things in a certain way provides an opportunity for an industry practitioner to re-examine his or her approach to particular tasks. So the lecturers were also learning, as were the people running it! The ever-evolving nature of the industry meant that lecturers almost had to alter their lecture from year to year merely to take those changes into account.

The course, in my view was invaluable in short-circuiting the normal learning process, and it attracted numerous students who subsequently found work in the industry, including employment in the U2 office, Sony Music, IMRO, MCPS, *Hot Press,* MTV Europe, and elsewhere, not to mention those who went on to set up their own companies in PR or other arms of the industry.

Indeed, I take a little pride in knowing that for quite a while a certificate awarded to those who successfully completed the course hung on the walls in the offices of MTV Europe. The MIX Course is still running and is now managed by *Hot Press* after Jackie and I retired having overseen it for 10 years, and Suzanne is happily pursuing her ambitions, career and family life.

Chapter Eleven

CELTIC WOMAN - A BRAND NOT A BAND

Since leaving Clannad in 1990 I hadn't had a lot of business-related contact with Dave Kavanagh, although we met every now and then for a game of golf or a social event. I was aware of his various exploits since the Irish music business is a fairly close-knit community where very little goes unnoticed. He'd continued to manage Clannad, and they continued to be a major international force into the early 90s.

One day in 2004 he called and asked me to meet him to discuss a new project he was working on which was called Celtic Woman, a concept based around four superb female singers and an energetic fiddle player, as well as a choir and small orchestra. Dave then invited me to a special show before a sold-out attendance at the Helix Theatre on the north side of Dublin on September 15, 2004. There was an element of déjà vu in this, as it instantly recalled the day he'd asked me to listen to 'Harry's Game'.

Back then, the Irish music industry and the Irish music media were at best sceptical about how the Celtic Woman concept would work overseas, especially in America. To be truthful, and bearing in mind I only had the show's title to go on, I wasn't overly excited either. In the wake of the *Riverdance* success, several Irish-based extravaganzas were launched to great fanfares but to mixed success, although shows by the ex-*Riverdance* star Michael Flatley, The Celtic Tenors and The Irish Tenors all did exceptionally well, both at home and abroad.

But the Celtic Woman project was still regarded as a substantial risk, given the fickleness and unpredictability of the music-loving public, and the fact that this would be an expensive show to mount. Some of the girls knew each other by reputation and through casual meetings, but this was to be the first time the singers Chloe, Lisa, Meav, Orla and fiddle player Mairead had all performed together in public. To increase the pressure and the tension, they only had a minimum amount of rehearsal time.

Having seen the success of Dave's visionary approach in the past, I knew he wouldn't be risking his time and reputation on a folly, so I wasn't surprised when the quality of the stage set told me this was no ordinary show. As soon as I walked into the theatre, I was immediately struck by the elaborate stage setting, the quality of the sound, the designer dresses and the beautiful harmonies of the singers. I could also see there was a lot of money being spent as I counted the thirteen cameras being used to film the show. At the interval, I used an old showbiz trick. I mingled with the audience in the foyer and bar area and listened (overheard) to the audience's comments on what they'd seen and heard during the first half performance. This is one way a pro can gauge whether or not the show is working. The public are always the ultimate judges of any performance. In this instance, all the comments were very positive. Consequently, any residual misgivings I'd had about the show's potential were swept away, and the rollercoaster ride began again.

The show was primarily being filmed as a one-off programme for broadcast on public service television (PBS) in the USA. I could sense this show was specifically aimed at the Irish diaspora, although it was to grow way beyond that specific market. The repertoire consisted of a blend of established Irish songs and tunes, such as 'Danny Boy' and 'She Moved Thru The Fair', contemporary songs like Enya's 'Orinoco Flow' and Clannad's 'Harry's Game'. International hits of the calibre of 'Walking In The Air' and 'Someday', alongside specially-written material. I had a meeting with Dave later that week and he told me the feedback was so positive he was planning to send the show out as a live event in big American venues and asked if I'd be interested in handling the music publishing. I agreed, and to that end, we set up a new publishing company Liffey Publishing Ltd of which I would be the Managing Director and we agreed to run it in much the same way as I'd done with the Clannad Music catalogue. There was no doubt that even in music terms I'd come a long way since the Punk-inspired days with Scoff Records.

Dave hit on another shrewd move in that he would avoid focusing on any individual performer and make the show the star. This had worked for *Riverdance* producer Moya Doherty after she bravely parted company with Michael Flatley on the eve of that show's UK premiere, so lessons had been learned all round. We decided early on that Celtic Woman was a brand, not a band. None of the Celtic Women would get individual treatment and as such there would be no stars, and all would be treated (and paid!) equally. It was easy to understand that with the gruelling schedule the performing troupe and crew would have to undertake as they traversed the USA and beyond, it'd be virtually impossible to keep the team together indefinitely anyway. Such a schedule can be very demanding on individuals, perhaps even more so on relationships.

The Helix performance was subsequently broadcast on PBS in the USA in March 2005, and the Celtic Woman CD and DVD released. Such was the instant popularity of the project that on March 18, less than three weeks after the initial release, both releases were number one in their respective charts on the Amazon website. Suddenly, industry insiders began to take the project very seriously, amid mounting speculation that it could in time rival, if not surpass, the achievements of *Riverdance*. And that was only the beginning. The CD album arrived straight into the number one slot in the *Billboard* 'World Music Charts' and reached number 22 in the same magazine's 'New Artist Chart', extraordinary success for a show that hadn't even existed six months previously. These achievements were reinforced on June 30 when nearly 200 Public Broadcasting Stations, of which there is at least one in nearly every state of the USA, broadcast the Celtic Woman show.

Mid-July saw the unveiling of the Celtic Woman live show to an enthusiastic audience at a concert in Cleveland, Ohio. This was followed by 18 successful concerts as the music-loving public took the girls, the show and the songs to their collective bosom, proof that the Celtic Woman franchise was about more than recording pristine CDs and DVDs and they could deliver the goods in live settings too. Over the years I've seen many memorable Celtic Woman shows in various parts of the USA, venues like Radio City in New York, the magnificent Red Rocks amphitheater in Colorado, Slane Castle and Powerscourt in Ireland, as well as in Zurich, Switzerland, and have always been impressed by the warmth of the audience reaction. I suspect that filling Radio City on two snow-bound nights convinced me that Celtic Woman was an unstoppable winner. I remember at the interval going across to the merchandise stand and seeing crowds' queueing to buy t-shirts, posters, badges, CDs, DVDs and so on or 'merch' as we call it in the trade.

There has been something like 14 changes in the line-up which were initially resisted by the hardcore fans, but in time they accepted those changes. Some singers have left to pursue solo careers, as is their right, but it's puzzled me over the decades to see individuals leaving successful ensembles to go solo and then fail. I know musicians and singers are often driven by their artistic ambitions, and it's arguable that all successful artists must have that drive, otherwise they might all have given up just as I, and many who were far more talented than me, did all those years ago. It's worth noting that some singers left but later rejoined when their circumstances changed. But when a frontline vocalist decides to move on from Celtic Woman, much consideration goes into choosing a replacement. This is the job of the musical director (MD) who puts the aspiring members through their paces. It's not just a question of finding someone with a lovely voice, but, because so much of the show's work is harmony-based, that new voice has to blend seamlessly with the others and of course get on with their fellow cast members and musicians.

I'd gotten a taste of the life of a performer during my own, somewhat limited, musical career. I know that rush of adrenaline you get from a cheering audience reaction, and I can understand why some performers become addicted to it. Perhaps it's the pursuit of that buzz that entices members of successful bands to leave to pursue solo careers as that would, in theory at least, put them closer to centre stage and slap-bang in the eye of the spotlight. Some, of course, have made it work, but many flounder on their own as if they've strayed too far from the mothership. They may have convinced themselves that the acclaim they received in the previous line-up would be replicated when they performed solo, or that blind self-belief would be enough to get them through, but these are false assumptions.

Many acts are actually successful because of some indefinable magical chemistry between the personalities; The Beatles are a terrific example of that. Ringo Starr mightn't have been the best drummer on the planet, but The Beatles with a technically better drummer mightn't have had that magic mix of ingredients and balance of personalities that endeared them to millions the world over.

It's not all down to having the right singers either. As any fan will understand, choosing the right songs is another key factor in the success of Celtic Woman or any show of its kind. And you can't simply pick a bunch of tunes at random and say, 'There's two dozen fairly decent songs, they'll do'. At the top level at which Celtic Woman works, considerable thought must go into the selection of each and every song. Nearly all shows are competing with numerous other shows, and each one is striving to do whatever it takes to gain a little edge over their rivals, so the nonchalant approach is out from the start.

As experienced musicians and serious music fans realise, a show is a delicate balance of light and shade, and a variety of moods and tempos, and placing the right song in the wrong place can totally upset the natural flow of any musical experience. But all that responsibility is ultimately in the hands of the show's owner, Dave, and the musical director, show producer etc. Dave, as usual, had assembled a top class professional group of people which I was very happy to be included in.

As with Clannad, and many other fine live acts before them, the public only see the 90/120 minutes of the show on stage but have very little notion of what goes on behind the scenes. Aspiring performers only see the stage shows and maybe bits on television and think, 'That looks easy. That looks like a handy way to earn a living. I'll have some of that'! But there's an art in the way so many acts can make it all look easy and effortless. Indeed, when it comes to the show, regardless of their mood or state of mind or whatever personal worries they might have in their private lives, the act has to get on that stage and make something magical happen for the people who've paid good money for tickets and travelled from far and wide at considerable expense. So the performers are always under pressure to deliver according to the audience expectations. For the performer, it might be the 29th concert of that tour, but for the vast bulk of the audience, this is a very special one-off night. There must be nights when the performer would prefer to be free to go for a walk or spend time with friends or visit a favourite restaurant, but they can't. Musicians have told me that as soon as the show starts they get something like an adrenalin rush and they switch into a different world where only they and the audience exist. I've often thought the role of the performer is more like a vocation or a way of life rather than a career.

It's been claimed that some become addicted to the high they get from performing and the affection they feel from the audiences. It never happened with Celtic Woman or Clannad, but if a show is poorly attended, like it or not the act still has to turn it on for the 20 people who've paid to see them. Spare me those acts, and I've observed too many of them over the years, who arrive at a venue and refuse to play because only a small number of people have turned up to see them.

When an inspiring figurehead like Bob Geldof said, on launching The Boomtown Rats, that all he wanted was, 'to get rich, get famous and get laid' he was probably speaking to many who'd like to do exactly that, but who simply didn't have the commitment, drive and the capacity for sheer hard work like Geldof had. That's why I'm not a big fan of TV talent shows, such as *The X-Factor,* or *Britain's Got Talent* etc., because they make it seem like success comes relatively easy, you're totally obscure one week and a couple of weeks later you're a national celebrity on the front pages of all the tabloids and hiding from the paparazzi. I can't help suspecting that such shows are exploiting the dreams of young people in a way that disregards how those kids might deal with rejection from the general public and returning to obscurity, as most of them inevitably do.

Little do most young and impressionable wannabes know how hard most artists work, even many unsuccessful ones, not to mention the team working behind the scenes, and the drudgery of hanging around airports, hotel rooms, TV studios and recording studios, travelling endless miles on the bus, checking in and out of hotels, packing and unpacking. Add to that the daily grind of the sound check, rehearsals and interviews for the various media, many of who ask the same questions again and again, and that's a long way from the image people have of what that life is really like.

When a show is over and the fans go home, or for a drink or a meal, the artists may have to stay around to meet and greet fans, sign autographs, pose for photos and so on, perhaps not getting to their hotel room until the early hours of the morning. Meanwhile, the crew must dismantle the gear, carefully pack it in trucks and begin the drive through the night to the next concert venue where they'll do it all over again, like a Groundhog Day that lasts for weeks, even months!

Most tours are planned with military precision, with every member of the crew and band given a schedule of each day's activities and timings. It only works if everybody follows instructions to the letter, as one person arriving late for a tour-bus departure can jeopardize plans for that day and might even put an entire tour at risk. One Celtic Woman tour manager, a real tough lady from Dublin, operated what she called the 'oil-spot,' policy. In other words, if you were late for the tour bus departure you were left with nothing but the oil spot indicating where the bus had been, and you'd have to make your own way to the next destination. Human nature being what it is, if you tolerate one person being late, the next day it's someone else and discipline falls apart. At its height, the Celtic Woman touring show and crew numbered 48 people and cost about $200, 000 per week to keep on the road so you can imagine how necessary total professional discipline was to the operation.

When I arrived in Zurich to see Celtic Woman I found them mid-morning at the venue rehearsing a tune which had obviously developed a few quirks that needed ironing out. So an enormous amount of work takes place away from the spotlight. Fortunately for me, my work was mostly carried out far away from the spotlight, and despite seeing wonderfully exciting shows over the years I've never for a second hankered to return to my former non-career as a singer. To stand at the back of a venue like the Royal Albert Hall in London or Sydney Opera House and know you were part of the intimate team who put the show together that the audience was clearly enjoying brought enormous satisfaction. I enjoyed the responsibility of taking the necessary steps to ensure all legally required copyright credits, permissions and paperwork were well in hand ahead of each release and performance. The copyright owners of all songs recorded and performed by Celtic Woman have to be accurately credited, so the appropriate royalties are paid.

2016 Celtic Woman rehearsals, Kilkenny

There are serious legal implications around issues of copyright, but there are also personal considerations that have to be taken into account. Nobody who has written a song wants to see that work wrongly attributed to another songwriter, no matter how innocently that mistake might have occurred. Sometimes it's very easy to trace the copyright owners of a particular song, especially a contemporary composition such as 'Orinoco Flow' recorded and co-written by Enya in the 1980s. But in the case of older songs, it can often be much more complex and can be made even more confusing when past recordings of an old song have had incorrect publishing and/or composer credits printed on the record sleeve or on the record label itself. Resolving such complications involves thorough, and often time-consuming, research in order to obtain the correct details.

Furthermore, the similarity between titles can add to the confusion. For example, some performers have assumed that the song, 'Isle of Innisfree', also spelt

Inisfree, has some links with the popular, W. B. Yeats poem 'The Lake Isle of Innisfree'. In fact, we initially made that error ourselves, but subsequently corrected it and attributed the song to its rightful author Dick Farrelly.

There's the added complication that compositions can be assigned to different publishing companies in different countries, so I needed to check the credits for every country in which we wanted to issue Celtic Woman DVDs and CDs or where we wanted to present the Celtic Woman show. This is what made my work on Celtic Woman so fascinating, and might explain why, years after I was initially invited on board, the show is still filling arenas all across America.

The show tours for about eight months in the USA every year and indeed, Celtic Woman has had the honour of performing in the White House for two American Presidents, President Bill Clinton and President Barack Obama. They've also performed in many other countries around the world including Australia, Japan, Brazil, South Africa and the UK.

Nor did our adventures stop at Celtic Woman. It's a fairly routine procedure that when you have a successful act you want to build on that success and expand the company's activities, just like when we were flying high with Clannad and we signed the Wexford band Cry Before Dawn.

So one day in the Liffey office I was having a brainstorming session with Dave when he asked me, 'Johnny, what was the first Irish band to make it really big in America?' I thought about it for a while and answered, 'That would have to be The Clancy Brothers and Tommy Makem, Dave.' They were a legendary ballad group who were enormously popular in the USA in the sixties and were an inspiration to budding folk acts of the time, including Bob Dylan who later described Liam Clancy as the best ballad singer ever.

This sowed the seed for our attempt to put together a top-notch act who'd become a Clancy Brothers for the new millennium with a clear focus on the US market. And thus in 2006, we created The High Kings, a band with a truly awe-inspiring pedigree whose members are all significantly successful in their own right. My early fondness for the Clancy Brothers stood me in good stead and the line-up included Finbarr Clancy (son of the late Bobby Clancy who'd been a member of The Clancy Brothers). Also on board were Martin

Furey, (son of Finbar from the famous Fureys group), Brian Dunphy, (son of the popular Irish singer Sean Dunphy), and the highly-experienced Darren Holden.

Although Darren may not have come from a high-profile musical dynasty, he'd starred as 'The Piano Man' (Billy Joel) in the Tony Award-winning hit musical *Movin' Out* composed by Billy Joel and Twyla Tharp. So the line-up alone gave us an undeniably unique selling point, but the band was far more than your standard rough-around-the-edges ballad group. Instead, they brought a high level of sophistication to the music, with their especially warm harmonies, the general quality of their musicianship, natural good humour and their terrific stage presence and interaction. The show was enhanced with high production values, including a sizeable backing band, a screen onto which appropriate images were projected and an exciting bodhran duet. The show also included a segment where The High Kings performed a special Clancy Brothers medley, complete with Aran ganseys. This was all admirably captured on their first DVD recorded live at the world-famous Ardmore Studios in Bray, Co Wicklow.

Yes, as with virtually any new act it was hard work at the beginning, especially with people assuming they were just another ballad group until they saw them live or on TV or heard tracks from their fine albums. We quickly realised that the full-scale show was too expensive to tour, especially as the Irish ballad audience was narrower than the Celtic Woman audience and we scaled it down to focus exclusively on the four guys and they spent six months working in a studio with the renowned Shay Healy in order to polish their slimmed-down act while also ensuring the versions they did of popular ballads like, 'Step It Out Mary' carried the unique High Kings' stamp and avoided being just another traditional Irish band of which Ireland is chock-a-block.

So ours and their perseverance paid off, and at the time of writing this book they continue to build their profile in the USA and Europe, while touring Ireland on a regular basis and building sales of their numerous CD albums. They've done most of the important Irish festivals in the USA and have even been lauded by President Barack Obama following a performance in the White House. I'd put their success down to word of mouth because they put on the kind of show that sends fans home in a good mood and word gets around. They're also very popular with the kind of radio programme that specializes in folk music, and perform very well on TV too and make for articulate interviewees.

But you also have to be careful in marketing an act like The High Kings that you don't ghettoize them in the Irish folk market so that other markets ignore them. I think we managed to achieve that, probably through applying our shared experience working with previous acts.

In 2015, they reached an even broader audience when they were invited to represent Ireland on the official Rugby World Cup album which had them working on an updated version of Phil's Irish rugby anthem, 'Ireland's Call'. This was a major coup given the Rugby World Cup is one of the biggest sporting events in the world. The build-up to the centenary of the 1916 Easter Rising seemed to have rekindled interest in our musical heritage and that, in my opinion, has also attracted many to The High Kings. They've also added some of their own original songs to their live repertoire, and they seem to be hugely popular, especially with Irish and American audiences. It's truly heartening to see an idea that I was involved in generating one day in our office come to fruition so successfully on such an international level.

Chapter Twelve

WHAT'S ANOTHER EUROVISION

Although its impact has somewhat faded here in recent years, the annual Eurovision Song Contest, and the battle to select the song to represent Ireland, have been major events for the Irish music industry, as they have for artists and the general public alike. Even people whose interest in music might be fairly casual tend to make a date with Eurovision every year, and Eurovision parties are common throughout Ireland and beyond.

Ireland's wonderful track record in the event has been well-documented, and I can well remember Dana's ground-breaking victory with 'All Kinds Of Everything' in 1970. The record went to number one in several countries, including Ireland and the UK, an outcome that would be unlikely for a Eurovision victor today. Johnny Logan won it again for us in 1980 with Shay Healy's terrific song 'What's Another Year', so in 1981 it was Ireland's turn to host the event. That meant a massive influx of delegates from all over Europe and elsewhere into Dublin for the week preceding the competition. There was something happening all day, every day during that week, including rehearsals, press conferences, receptions, official functions, parties and showcase gigs. So for an active partygoer like yours truly, it was a gruelling week! Each visiting country would usually host a reception in the evening during that week and on one particular night, there were four receptions one after the other. It's (sometimes) a tough job, but somebody's gotta do it!

Partying aside, the concept of Eurovision wasn't widely popular with rock music hipsters, including myself, so in Dublin 1981, Billy Magra and Smiley Bolger came up with the idea of holding an alternative Eurovision Song Contest event in McGonagles, a popular rock venue in Dublin's South Anne Street. Admission to the piss-take evening cost an old penny and only people from the music industry were allowed to perform. Being able to play an instrument wasn't compulsory. In spite of his previous triumph in the real contest, Shay Healy performed with his band, which for this occasion was named, Shay & The Royalties. I was a member of an outfit called The Rubbers, a knowing nod to the fact that contraceptives were still illegal in Ireland. We sang a version of Pink Floyd's then-recent hit single 'Another Brick in The Wall' which we crudely renamed 'Another Prick in The Dail' as a pointed jibe at the inhabitants of our parliament in Leinster House. Dave Kavanagh was our guitarist, and a one-armed guy named Marty, a friend of Dave's, played drums (long before Def Leppard did likewise). Tony Strickland, who ran Clannad's fan club, was dressed in a nappy (aka diaper) and was busily building a wall on the stage with cardboard boxes. I was the lead singer, dressed in a bulked-out body-stocking and equipped with a mortarboard and a cane. We distributed lots of condoms to the audience as a gesture of protest against the ridiculous ban the government of the time had imposed, and I waved my cane at the audience and demanded 'Show me your rubbers'. On cue, the audience waved their condoms back at the stage. We had a great laugh about that night for many years after.

I recall the adrenalin rush I felt following our eh, performance and thinking to myself, that must be what really attracts musicians and performers to the stage as it's a natural high which is incredibly intense, and I've also read about this from sporting professionals who experience the same thing. There were a surprising number of genuine Eurovision delegates in the audience. They had a good laugh and enjoyed what must've been a truly surreal experience, especially when one assumes they may have attended a black-tie government reception in Dublin Castle at some stage during the same week. All in all, just another hilarious night in the madcap Irish music industry!

On the serious side of Eurovision, I was several times on the judging panels that selected the Irish songs for our National Song Contest which in turn would choose Ireland's Eurovision entry. The annual process would begin with RTE inviting entries from Irish songwriters. They would usually convene four panels, each one probably consisting of a songwriter, a music publisher, a music journalist and their own representative. Each panel would be allotted maybe 100 song entries each, and the four panels would eventually whittle it down to 16 songs. RTE would then choose 8 of those songs and allot singers for the television show which might feature a different panel to choose our national entry.

I remember well our 1994 entry 'Rock and Roll Kids', written by Brendan Graham and performed by Charlie Mc Gettigan and Paul Harrington. I fancied it at the RTE judging stage and later had a few bob on the song when it went into the competition proper, which it duly won! (Result for all of us!) That system seemed to work well for Ireland, and it wasn't until the public were charged with the voting that we (Ireland) started to perform worse in the competition's finals.

Maybe that's just a coincidence, but I reckon it's difficult enough for an experienced professional to judge a song, and I'm not convinced members of the public can listen to a song without being distracted by other factors, such as the quality of the singer, the stage presentation, the singer's demeanour or hairstyle or fashion awareness, or even the band line-up.

As a seasoned professional, I confess I can be distracted from attending to the core of the song itself which we're supposed to be judging and I have to work my attention back to that. So while I understand it's wonderful for the public involved, I'm not sure if it moves the event away from being a pure song contest as such.

Another change came when the Eurovision organisers decided to stop having an orchestra to back each singer and allowed backing tracks to be used. From that point on, the focus seemed to switch to acts putting on the most exciting stage displays, and once again the song itself faded into the background. There are strict rules such as no country can have more than six performers on stage, so over the years the performing acts have gotten more imaginative by introducing grandmothers, cement mixers, bizarre costumes, distinctive hairstyles (think Jedward) etc. which, of course, again distract from the fact that it's a SONG competition.

But all of that came after Linda Martin won for Ireland in 1992 with 'Why Me'. And the 1993 event, broadcast live from the Green Glens venue in Millstreet, Co Cork, is reputed to have attracted an audience of 350 million who saw Niamh Kavanagh triumph for Ireland with 'In Your Eyes'.

I was a guest at an après-contest reception in the Gleneagles Hotel in nearby Killarney. It was about 3am and I was talking to the very well known & colourful owner when a Garda came in. The place was still heaving, the bar was still open, and it seemed like all of Europe was there celebrating, even if it was well after licensing hours. The Garda walked up to the proprietor and said:-

'Jesus Christ, you can't have a bar open at this hour of the morning.' The hotel owner knew the Garda and said, 'You know, Guard, you're absolutely right. Now if I were you I'd go around and take the names of every one of the people here (about 2,000) and we'll have the biggest court case in Kerry history!' The Garda looked around again, decided he wasn't going to win on this occasion and left, maybe to have a pint himself for all I know.

But Eurovision has changed and I would argue not for the better from a music publisher's perspective. When Lordi won for Finland in 2006, they were dressed as lizards and used chainsaws. Add in the suspicion that politics affects votes and it's no surprise that many are calling for a complete re-think of the entire contest and its structure.

As well as the public having a say in selecting the Irish entry, RTE have tried involving mentors for the Irish finalists but with mixed success. In a way, we might need to bow to reality, revise our assumptions about the contest and accept it as a visual spectacle, with the song having less significance in the overall plan.

There was a time when a Eurovision winner like Abba's 'Waterloo' or Bucks Fizz 'Making Your Mind Up' would sell upwards of 100,000 records in Ireland and possibly a million all over Europe. As soon as the finalists were announced in one country music publishers would strive to sign up any song they thought had a real chance of overall victory. In one year CBS signed five of the eight finalists in the Irish part of the event which was won by Cathal

Dunne with 'Happy Man'. Now the winning entry barely troubles the charts anywhere.

Anyway, long may the Eurovision parties continue. It's just entertainment, folks!

Chapter Thirteen

VERSE, CHORUS, HOOK -
WHAT MAKES A HIT SONG?

Because the natural state of the music industry is one of permanent change, you can never rest on your laurels and assume you know it all. This applies just as acutely to music publishing and to the songs we publish. Every day you learn something new about even the most popular songs. For example, while most people assume 'Danny Boy' is an old Irish song from centuries past, at least parts of the words in some versions were composed by Fred Weatherly who wasn't Irish at all. He was an English lawyer who passed away in 1929, and since the copyright currently expires 70 years after the death of the writer, that song, including his contribution, is now out of copyright. But somebody unaware of Weatherly's death mightn't know this.

For another, more obvious, example you could consider songs written, or partly written, by John Lennon. He was tragically assassinated in 1980, and any royalties accruing from his songs currently go to his heirs. But under present copyright legislation, in 2050 anyone will be able to arrange his songs and claim Lennon's share of the copyright for themselves. So although Lennon is dead, his estate still holds the copyright in his songs in conjunction with the music publisher to whom they're assigned. No wonder I sometimes feel the job I do is more like that of a musical detective!

Songs to me are the raw materials of the music industry, no songs, no industry! So I have good cause to be thankful to those songwriters and composers without whom I wouldn't have had the challenging life I've had. Then again, if I had a Euro for every time I've been asked to explain what makes a hit song…

Although we usually find it impossible to explain why songs can have a deep, and often very personal, effect on us as individuals and that applies to music industry practitioners just as easily as it does to fans. Our favourite pieces of music form a soundtrack to our lives and the best of them can survive all kinds of different versions, including a tired and emotional Uncle Harry and Aunt Vera 'having a go' in the small hours after somebody's wedding.

Equally, song verses can have different meanings to different listeners. I've watched parties of women sing lustily along to Tom Jones' hit 'Delilah' as if unaware that it's a tragic song about a man stabbing his woman to death. People can take great delight in singing a song about a very dark subject, or, for all I know, may in a few cases harbour remote fantasies about doing something similar. But maybe it's also ok that it's just a catchy song with a strong 'hook' line. Never mind the general public, I also wonder if every professional musician who sings 'Nessun Dorma' knows what the Italian words mean? (FYI: No One Sleeps)

There are verses in songs that not even the songwriter can explain the meaning of, and still, it doesn't matter. I've heard fans sing totally wrong lyrics to songs they only know the melodies of. So sometimes it's not all of the song that matters, and the appeal is in the catchy chorus, an emotive line, the storytelling, or the mood created by the combination of melody, words and performer. Most music fans will recall those moments when we recognise the opening bars of a pet song and are immediately transported back to the time we first heard it, perhaps decades before.

But a great song not only transcends the decades but can move easily across genres. The Beatles' version of 'Yesterday' is a light, classically-tinged pop song, but in Ray Charles version it's transformed into a heart-achingly beautiful soul ballad. That song can shine when played by orchestras, string quartets, jazz combos and just about any artist who can hold a melody. (Although, I'm in no hurry to hear the improvised version by Bob Dylan and George Harrison ever again!)

I remember once reading what the English author Somerset Maugham said about novels- 'there are just three rules for writing a novel, unfortunately, no one knows what they are!' You could say the same about songwriting.

I'm not going to argue that anybody can write a song, but it's a common skill and once learned it's rarely forgotten. I genuinely feel that emerging songwriters are almost totally unaware of the number of songwriters already established and the number of wannabes also struggling for a piece of the action. Yes, the song you've just written might become an international standard, or it might just be one more song added to the billions that already exist. An experienced songwriter could arguably take a week and dash off half a dozen decent songs, and who knows, one or two of them might be killers. But at the very least they'd achieve a basic minimum standard.

But what the music publisher is trying to spot is the one that stands out and has something extra-special about it, and that's not easy. After all, if I knew the magic formula I'd write songs myself! That said I believe there are basic guidelines, I won't describe them as rules, that help a song make an impression in the commercial world.

For example, if you write a song that needs a 50-second intro that might not help it get plays on the radio where they generally need recordings to get to the point fairly quickly, say what they have to say and move on. There's a general acceptance in the business, if you can't grab the listener in the first 30 seconds you'll probably struggle to do so for the remainder of the song.

Personally, I like a song to have a neat, crisp intro lasting about 15 seconds. It also helps if the chorus or hook-line comes in fairly early, perhaps in less than a minute, and is repeated as often as the structure of the song will bear. Sometimes that's all people remember of a song. A good example is Paul Simon's 'The Boxer'. I've seen audiences respond only to the part that goes 'lie-la-lie, lie-la-la-la-lie-lie, lie-la-lie, lie-la-la-la-la-lie-la-la-lie' and I'm not sure if they even know what the rest of the song is about. But that hook is irresistible and impossible to forget. Incidentally, it was Paul Simon who said you can have a hit with a song that has a great melody but average words, but not with a song that has great lyrics and an average melody. There's so much truth in that.

The length of a song is also a significant factor when it comes to radio play. I know some artists who lose plays because their songs are deemed too long, and I always advise writers that the core song works best if it works within a 3 or 4-minute span. Of course, there are exceptions that disprove every rule, and they tend to be the songs that are extra-special. The Beatles 'Hey Jude' is over 7 minutes long, but if it hadn't been by the Fab Four would it have even been listened to? Bob Dylan's 'Like A Rolling Stone' is 6 minutes long, and promotional copies of the single sent to radio stations had the song split over the two sides. But that was Bob Dylan. Would the record company have done it for Bob Murphy? Perhaps not.

There's no set formula for writing songs and there are many different types of songs. There are songs that tell a story, straightforward pop songs and even ones that have a musical hook as an intro (think Gerry Rafferty's 'Baker Street', with its instantly recognisable saxophone intro). One of the things I listen out for is whether the lyric can be interpreted with different meanings to different people or scenarios.

An artist like Barry White was well known for performing songs with lyrics that could mean vastly different things to many people. It's said that many babies were conceived to his music. Then again, he had a very seductive voice to go with his tunes! He sold over 100 million albums with songs like 'Can't Get Enough of Your Love, Babe' and 'You're the First, the Last my Everything' along with the likes of 'Never Never Gonna Give You Up' and 'Don't Make Me Wait Too Long' in his repertoire. Maybe he was the subject of Sade's 1984 hit song, 'Smooth Operator'. Who knows!

Barry died in 2003 but his songs, I suspect, will live forever, which is what every songwriter is trying to achieve with their music. One of the greatest (in my humble opinion) living songwriters is Paul Simon. He is now 77 years old and has been writing hit songs since the 1950's. He has written countless hits including 'Homeward Bound' (1966), 'The Boxer' (1968), 'Bridge over Troubled Water' (1969) along with personal favourites of mine '50 Ways to Leave Your Lover' (1975) and 'You Can Call Me Al' (1986). His lyrics, (which I can't quote for copyright reasons!) are legendary. Oh! And that clever man owns ALL his own publishing through his company Paul Simon Music, which I believe is now administered through one of the world's biggest publishing companies, Universal Music.

I recall the writer Phil Coulter once being asked in a television interview what it took to succeed in the music business as an artist? He replied that, 'talent is only your ticket into the game.' It's so true. It's a combination of being in the right place at the right time, with the right product, a good team, and a good sprinkling of luck.

Chapter Fourteen

NORTH DAKOTA

The 25th February 1995, was a date that would change the direction of my life. I was sitting at a bar in a popular Dublin nightclub (as you do) called Joys. Earlier that evening, around 9 pm, I'd attended a launch or reception for some new record, the details of which escape me. I'd been accompanied by two friends Tommy Walsh from the band Speranza (whom I published at the time) and Grainne O' Brien who handled the band's PR, and we'd retired to Joys for some late-night refreshment. The club was renowned as a drinking hole for politicians and businessmen looking for after-hours fun. Tommy and Grainne split at about 1.30am for another venue but, unusually for me, I decided to stay on. So I sat at the bar with an empty chair either side of me and an almost full bottle of wine in front of me.

At about 2am two very attractive blonde women arrived up to the bar and, naturally (lol), I asked if they'd like a drink. They looked at me skeptically, but accepted and we introduced ourselves. One of the two girls was Colette Rooney and during the course of conversation I learned she was a civil servant. The other lady was Maureen and she worked at the perfume counter in Arnotts, a well-known Dublin department store. All three of us chatted for a while until Maureen was hustled onto the dance floor leaving Colette and myself alone. She looked at me and said, 'Do me a favour, please don't tell me what you do for a living'. I said, 'No problem'. And so we talked and the first coincidence we noticed was that both of us had just come out of serious relationships on the very same day the previous month. She after a four year one and me from the aforementioned young lady after my Australian sojourn.

We were getting on well and I suggested we head on to another late-night haunt run by the affable female impersonator Mr Pussy (Alan Amsby). This was a basement type venue called Mr Pussy's Café De Lux a cabaret and private club in Suffolk St, Dublin which was small and intimate and was quietly supported by Bono and movie director Jim Sheridan. The club served white tea or red tea in china cups, or mugs for the more thirsty patrons, while Mr Pussy himself conducted the entertainment. The teas, of course, were white and red wine... this club operated on a need to know basis, so they were very selective as to who got in, and as it happened Grainne & Tommy had also gone to the club earlier. Colette and Grainne were getting along famously, and she assured Colette I was a sound guy with no sinister intentions! As it turned out we chatted until the club closed for the night and we were politely ushered to the exit.

Having imbibed several helpings of tea, I picked up the courage to ask Colette if she'd fancy coming back to my place. She looked me straight in the eye and said, 'No. Would you fancy coming back to mine?' To which I, naturally, agreed. This decision was to be the start of a relationship and later marriage, which has lasted for over 23 years (and counting). Colette had a lovely artisan cottage in Glasnevin on Dublin's north side. When we arrived at her place, she went to the stereo and played a Lyle Lovett track 'North Dakota' which Lyle released in 1992, but it wasn't very well known and was certainly seldom heard on Irish radio. This was also one of my favourite songs. (Remember, she didn't know what I did for a living). This song and other selections was a pleasant surprise and made me all the more curious about this lady....

After what could only be described as a whirlwind romance, I moved in with Colette on March 10th, about 13 days after we met. There'd always been a joking rivalry between the Southside and the Northside of Dublin city and we teased each other constantly about this. I'd say that- 'I finally got my passport stamped' when I moved over to Glasnevin. I was 45 years old and she 34. Both of us had also been married before, and knew all the pitfalls, but we both felt it was just the right thing for us to do.

Over time we discovered some more weird coincidences such as she was the third Colette Rooney I knew. Her family doctor was called John Lappin (whose son was also John), and whose practice was in Fairview on the Northside of Dublin. Later on, she told me that many years before while 'playing' on an Ouija board she'd gotten a message that the man she would end up with would be the 3rd John in her life!! All true, the 1st, her lifelong friend and the 2nd, her first husband. We also discovered we hung around the same pubs and clubs over previous years, so much so it was a wonder we hadn't met each other sooner. I had, of course, by this time told her, I worked as a music publisher, which took a bit of explaining (as it does to most people). Of course, I also (stupidly) told her of my painting & decorating background and soon found myself painting the cottage front to back!

She and her family were also quite musical and one of the first records she'd bought (and still has to this day) was Clannad's *In A Lifetime*. Our music tastes were bizarrely similar.

A few years ago we had Steve Cooney, a maestro on the didgeridoo, at our home for a visit. During the course of the conversation it came out that Steve had written a brilliant track called 'Skidoo', whereupon Colette left the room and returned with the original single and showed it to Steve. He was astonished to see it, saying he hadn't seen this single in years. He kindly signed a lovely message for Colette on it.

At the time I met Colette she worked in the Land Registry, having returned to Dublin after living in Galway for 5 years working in various administrative jobs. Colette is a really good administrator and as my business got busy, it seemed natural for us to work together. So, after a couple of years, she took a career break from the service and worked with me on royalty statements, contracts and general administration work. She also helped me with personal matters such as wardrobe, style, appearance and image as she had a natural eye for design which is most important in the music game. Likewise, I'm a pathetic cook, whereas Colette's a great one, and her culinary skills have kept me alive and in good health given the unhealthy rock'n'roll lifestyle and diet I'd indulged in over the previous crazy decades.

Back then, it was popular for bands and musicians to have receptions to launch their new singles or albums, and I'd often pick Colette up after work and we'd attend many such events together in those early days. She learned very quickly what the work of a publisher entailed, and what the music biz life was like. We happily lived and worked in Glasnevin until we found our beautiful home in the Wexford town of Enniscorthy where we moved in 1998. She never returned to the Civil Service! But then she was never a very 'civil servant' in the first place!

Chapter Fifteen

FAMILY, WORK, BUSINESS AND PLEASURE

There were two distinct characteristics at play in the Lappin family as I was growing up. My Mother had artistic leanings while my Dad was very much the businessman. It's fascinating to reflect, that working in the music industry, I'm straddling both.

Because Joan and Peggy caught the theatre bug, and because they were so much older than me, I didn't really have a normal brother-sister relationship with either of them, although we always got on extremely well any time we crossed paths. Des took a different approach, mixing the business side with my Mother's fondness for alcohol until his untimely death at the age of 37. Peggy and her husband went into the hotel business and had a very busy life. She was later estranged from her husband and died of cancer on Bastille Day in 2006 when she was 70 years of age, leaving Joan as my only living sibling.

Peggy had a terrific sense of humour even when she was terminally ill. I once went to visit her in St Francis Hospice in Raheny, where they lovingly care for the dying, and her first question was, 'Did you bring me any whiskey?' The staff was horrified by her suggestion, and I reminded her she was in a hospice, where bringing in whiskey was taboo. One day she actually got out of bed, got dressed and insisted I bring her to an off-license she knew was located around the corner!

On another occasion she told me she wanted to be cremated-

I said, 'Peggy, where would you like us to scatter your ashes?' She replied,

'I'd like you to scatter them in the Liffey flowing north.' (She was referring to the fact that she was born north of the border). I said to her, 'Peggy, I can do a lot of things, but making the Liffey flow north is a little beyond even *my* capability!' Colette asked her, 'How about a river in Portadown?' and she said, 'The River Bann', so we scattered her ashes in the Bann River in Portadown instead. A very strange thing happened at that small ceremony. There were about 6 family members present and when we all threw flowers into the river, they floated into the middle of the river and formed a perfect P…. I'll never forget that!

Joan and Liam had moved down to Bunclody, Co Wexford and soon after, I moved to Enniscorthy which is also in the South-East of Ireland. But I tended to see more of their daughter Leslie for the simple reason that she too had carved out a career for herself in the music business, first with the rock band In Tua Nua and later as a solo artist. Joan gave up acting when she got married, but still seems to have the stage in her blood and she might even harbour a regret or two that she didn't get to devote more time to it. She was deeply interested in Leslie's performing career and attended many of her concerts, and maybe she channelled her enthusiasm and love for performing into her daughter. When their son Barrie, who is in the movie business, was making a film about the notorious outlaw Ned Kelly in Australia, both Joan and Liam went out there for two months and worked in the wardrobe and costume department for Barrie.

Liam had artistic leanings himself and was known as a very natty dresser. He owned a number of electrical retail shops in the south east area which won several awards for design. Liam had a very creative eye for shop displays. He was also good with his hands and created many of the garden features and furniture items they have in their beautiful house in Wexford. He died in 2010.

My first wife Cathy continued to have health issues all through her life and she never re-married after we split up. I'm glad to say she's quite well now. Suzanne enjoyed a successful career in the insurance business, but she was always captivated by the work that I did and I often brought her to RTE if I had a band performing on the *Late Late Show* or some other programme.

So on one occasion when she was a young adult she phoned to ask if she could meet me to discuss something. When we met she told me she'd gone into a recording studio and recorded a demo tape of her singing a cover* song.

In one sense I was quite relieved she wasn't here to tell me she was pregnant, but on the other hand I wasn't convinced she had the talent to make a go of it in the music business as a performer and was merely getting caught up in the fever surrounding TV talent shows. When I listened to her recording those suspicions were confirmed. It was blatantly clear to me that Suzanne was not a singer. She asked me what I thought of her demo and I said, 'Suzanne, you CAN'T sing'. She wanted to go back to the studio and remake the demo, but I managed to convince her that no matter what she did with it she wasn't going to have a career as a pop singer because, as I told her, 'Suzanne, you couldn't carry a tune in a bucket'. Harsh, but true!

Eventually she believed me and parked that particular ambition. She got on with her other plans, including sowing the seeds for the MIX Course as I've already outlined, so she did achieve her ambition to work in the music industry, albeit in a slightly different way from how she'd envisaged it. More recently she became a certified affiliate partner for Jordan Belfort's *(The Wolf of Wall Street)* Straight Line Sales System, not surprisingly as she's a fine saleswoman and works well with people. She now works in the airline business as a flight attendant working the international routes from Dublin to New York and LA. Four thousand applied for two hundred places available and she got one of them. I believe she got her forthrightness and persistence from me and her patience from her Mother. And, she still can't sing!

My son Jonathan has been equally successful in the computer industry. He worked with multi-national giants Microsoft for nearly two decades in their Dublin HQ and has recently relocated to Brisbane in Australia where he's enjoying life as an IT specialist and consultant in that beautiful part of the world. I believe working in another country with a different cultural atmosphere can only be beneficial in the long run.

I've been working from my home office in Enniscorthy where I've lived with Colette since 1998. Having visited friends in Killinick, County Wexford and been impressed with the peace and the natural surroundings, a move to a different life in the south-east made sense. The fact that the traffic was becoming an increasing nightmare in Dublin was an added factor. I'm a bit of a stickler when it comes to punctuality, so this was stressing me out to the point that I was concerned for my wellbeing. The development of the Internet would enable me to do most of my work from home anyway, so it hardly mattered where I worked. I've always been thankful for this, being aware had I opted to stay in retail, for example, I'd have had to commute daily to a workplace. The time and energy saved can be better directed to more constructive matters.

Besides, Enniscorthy is only about 70 miles from Dublin and the road has improved substantially since I moved south. There's a major new bypass due to open in 2019 which will allow me to get to Dublin Airport in less than an hour and a half.

The traffic in Dublin had become increasingly worse during the Celtic Tiger madness, and I discovered I could get from Enniscorthy to, say, Dun Laoghaire, quicker than I used to commute from Glasnevin on one side of Dublin to Dun Laoghaire on the other.

Working from home also means I'm less subject to the distraction of others in the company dropping by the office to exchange the latest industry gossip or share their anxieties about one matter or another. I appreciate this kind of home-based set-up might not suit those who need the sense of comradeship and social connection you get in an office, but I tend to work well to deadlines and can concentrate better when I'm on my own. There was a stigma once attached to working from home, the implication being that you weren't really working at all, or didn't have a proper job. That's all changed, most probably because of computerisation. I remember talking to Paul McGuinness on the subject once (he had a beautiful home in Wicklow) and it didn't suit him at all because he found he was being distracted by the television, the radio and other things. And if there are no distractions you can create them. You make yourself a cup of tea, then a while later you fancy a coffee, or a yogurt, or a sandwich, or a quick look at the TV news, or maybe a listen to that new demo from Jill Bloggs, or even call a friend. You can actually squander an entire day not working if you really want to, hence the need for discipline and order.

I've always been an early-morning person, so I can start work as early as 6am, or even get up in the middle of the night to work on something that might be on my mind. But I usually start each day with what I call my 'thinking cigarette' when I start to focus on the key things I have to work on that day. I've smoked since I was 15 years old, and I've always said if I could change one thing about my life, I would never have started smoking. But hey, nicotine is one of the most addictive substances and I've never managed to kick the 'habit' (unfortunately). I hate it, but I'm stuck with it.

I've noticed I get quite a lot done between 6 am and 9 am because offices in Ireland generally open around 9 am. Given the detailed nature of some of the work, on royalty statements, for example, or dealing with international synchronisation rights*, it's good to have that comparatively quiet time to concentrate, as I'm fully aware a decimal point in the wrong place could be costly. My head is also reasonably uncluttered at that time of the day, although that can change later!

I can organise my day so as to fit personal chores in whenever I can, and the advent of the smart phones, tablets and computers have greatly freed home office workers from their previous desk-bound routines. There's very little of the detail of my work I can't do online, including the registration of songs, for example, and I have access to information about music publishing that enhances the way I do my work.

The music industry has very few jobs that you can do from 9 to 5. Record company scouts have to go to gigs in the evenings, because that's when they're on. Music reviewers must do likewise. Road crews work when the gigs are on. Record producers often work right through the night. A music publicist has to be aware of all the radio and TV shows on the main channels around the clock so they know which programmes their clients work might fit into. You couldn't do this work, even badly, if you wanted to clock on at 9 and off at 5 and keep the rest of the time for yourself and your other interests. You'd very quickly fall out of touch and slip from view. As I often say about the music business – 'We never close'.

The anti-social hours musicians and others work can put a major strain on relationships, as happened in my own situation with a woman who didn't want me to go to Australia to do my job. It's often particularly hard for female artists, especially those who want to raise a family or whose partner is holding down a post back home. In the years we've enjoyed of Celtic Woman we've had 12 different lead singers who've come and gone as other life demands took over.

The invention of the Internet and the ubiquity of mobile phones mean the job is non-stop around the clock, as it is for most people working in an international industry. While Europe is sleeping North and South America are moving into action, and when they call it a day, the Far East awakens. It can be a rarity to get through a full night's sleep without at least one phone call or email, WhatsApp message from overseas, and that call might rouse you from sleep and require you to get up and check a detail on a document or e-mail a piece of information or any number of requirements.

And it's not just Monday to Friday either, but the whole seven days. For example, one recent Easter Saturday my phone pinged, and although it was a bank holiday weekend, I hadn't risked turning it off. The call, as it happened, was from the *David Letterman Show* in the USA. They required instant clearance for a tune Rodrigo y Gabriella were going to perform on the show later that evening in New York.

A nine-to-fiver or a Monday-Friday operator wouldn't have been able to provide the necessary information, so the duo would've lost an important slot on one of the most viewed programmes in the USA. Furthermore, they might never have been invited back again. So that's why I have to keep my phone switched on, but even then I'm constantly struggling to keep abreast of what's going on in what's a very active business. But each person has to strike their own balance, and that's not always easy. Planning and efficiency are vital. I keep a diary and write down everything I have to do, and that enables me to slot in social events around the work load.

In a way, having, say, 20 songwriter clients is akin to having 20 different jobs, each one of which wants you to regard it as your priority. That's manageable, but only if you organise your life and work schedule to cope with it. Maybe that pressure provides an adrenalin rush which gets me through and keeps me going.

Yes, it's wonderful to be invited to after-show parties and receptions and glamorous lunches, and get more free CDs and concert tickets than you have time to use, but it's like the guy who got a job in a chocolate factory to the envy of all his mates. After a few weeks the novelty wore off and he might as well have been working in any factory making any product. Fortunately, the ever-changing nature of the music business keeps it fresh for all of us.

Although there's a widespread view that people who work in the business side of music have no interest in the music but are merely interested in making money, I personally found this to be almost totally untrue. When I meet any music industry colleague our conversation invariably revolves around music and the business. We'll talk about the new Ed Sheeran album or the U2 gigs or some emerging local act we've been impressed by. When I go for a private meal or to a bar I often try to find places where no music is played. Otherwise, my ears just naturally tune in to the background music and I get distracted in a way that can be very unfair on the company I'm in.

In fact, it can make your life a little claustrophobic, and that's why I've always tried to have friends who have nothing to do with the business and it's also why I've cultivated other interests, including golf and gardening. I remember when I started out in the 70s, some people would ask me why a Rock'n'Roller like myself who wore satin tour jackets and had long hair (Yes, I had hair once!) would indulge in such a sedentary game as golf! My standard answer was, 'Listen, I put a tee in the ground, I put a golf ball on the tee, I put all my worries and troubles into that golf ball and spend the next four hours hitting the ball as far away from me as I possibly can'.

That's been my therapy and one way of totally switching my mind off business matters. In a similar way, I'm fortunate enough to have a beautiful garden of almost an acre. Colette and I have spent the last twenty years building it, and love nothing more than pottering around it when the Sunny South East weather allows.

Sometimes, but not too often, I envy those like the shopkeeper who can shut up shop at 6 pm and head off to the cinema or go out for an uninterrupted meal or just have a quiet night with family and friends. But if I'd really wanted any of that so badly, I'd never have opted for a career in music, and despite my gripes I've never regretted it.

I've never actually been a salaried employee of any company in the music business, preferring to be a free agent as much as possible. The downside of working for yourself is the insecurity of not having a regular income, but being your own boss also means you can walk away from any situation that feels uncomfortable. So, I can rightfully claim, I've never had a job in my life!

Chapter Sixteen

LET THE GOOD TIMES ROLL - STORIES FROM THE VAULTS

In truth, I think anybody who's spent a reasonable (or even unreasonable) time in the entertainment business can tell a raft of stories, many of which arise out of a simple need to relieve the tedium of travel and hotel life. As Charlie Watts said of the first 25 years drumming with the Rolling Stones, it was five years of playing music and 20 years of hanging around. Yes, Charlie, life in the music business can be heavily time-consuming and stressful, facts that might explain why many of its practitioners look for a variety of ways to divert themselves from the daily grind and allow some space into their lives. Some find that diversion dabbling in illegal substances, while others take to the nightclubs, and I did my time in quite a few. I was an honorary member of many fine Dublin clubs like the Pink Elephant and Renards both celebrity hang-outs run by the irrepressible Mr. Robbie Fox.

THE DEMO & THE GLOVE

Such is the unreal nature of the music industry that bizarre things just happen, and not for no reason did Frank Zappa call it the industry of human happiness. During the early days at Scoff Records we were planning to release a record by a well-known band of the day called Auto Da Fe. The band featured the legendary Gay Woods and musicians of the calibre of Trevor

Knight. We arranged to record a demo of the song we were planning to release.

I'd known Phil Lynott for years and first saw him in the early 60's as a kid when he played in bands such as, The Black Eagles and later Skid Row. The first business name I used was JTF Promotions which was named after Lizzy's *Johnny The Fox* record. Yep, that's where the whole 'Fox' thing came from…

I asked Philo, as he was affectionately known in Dublin, if he'd do us (Scoff) a big favour and produce the Auto Da Fe demo. This, of course, would add huge credence to the record. Phil was like that, a lovely guy who was always ready to lend a hand and help up and coming local Irish musicians. He agreed and we booked time in Westland Recording Studios. On arriving at the studio to check on progress I asked the late Tim Martin, a legendary sound engineer who was in charge of the session, where Phil was.

Tim looked at me and said rather sheepishly, 'He's in the toilet Johnny'. I waited for about 15 minutes but there was still no sign of Phil emerging from the loo. Conscious that our tiny budget might be fast disappearing down the toilet, as it were, I went off to find him and find him I did, very generously, er… entertaining two nubile young ladies in the ladies toilet. You could say he was double-jobbing! Of course, he was lending his services to Scoff for free, so I was hardly in a position to take him to task. It was really all part of the sex, drugs and rock'n'roll lifestyle that many musicians bought into, although in Phil's case it had a tragic ending. But he was generous to me at the time, and I'll always remember him with affection, and the help he gave us in those early days.

He could be very funny too. When he formed the (supergroup) The Greedy Bastards with Gary Moore, Scott Gorham and Brian Downey from Thin Lizzy, and Steve Jones and Paul Cook (both from the Sex Pistols), they planned a gig at the ill-fated Stardust nightclub in Artane on the north side of Dublin in 1978. Philo was in the Scoff office one day telling myself and Deke and about the gig.

In my total naivety I asked him what kind of band they were. Were they, for instance, a folk band, I queried? Phil was wearing a leather glove with spikes on it at the time and he put this gloved hand up to my face and said,

'Johnny, does that look like a fuckin' folk band glove to you?' …I think I got the picture!

AN OCCASION AT THE CASTLE …. AND BEYOND

Back in 1981 Dave Kavanagh asked me to become involved with an open-air rock festival he was putting on over an August bank holiday weekend at the racecourse in Castlebar in Co Mayo. The Festival bill still looks impressive. It included Clannad, Chrissy Hynde with The Pretenders, Percy Sledge, Sonny Condell, Loudon Wainwright III, Ian Dury & The Blockheads, Freddie White and more. The event was given the rather grandiose title of, 'An Occasion at The Castle'.

We completely took over a hotel in the town where everybody involved in the festival were housed. Back then, there was a far more freewheelin' attitude to drugs like marijuana, and some of the musicians and members of their entourage no doubt, indulged as the fancy took them. One of the waiters serving our guests, as they wound down after the gig in the small hours, was very prissy and dressed immaculately in dickie bow and jacket, the lot. He inquired very politely about the cigarettes that seemed to exude a different smell from the cigarettes he was used to, so he asked if he could try one out.

Somebody duly obliged and he seemed to take to it straight away. Before long he began dropping the prim manner and dispensed with the dickie bow. Then he started giggling and shed the jacket too. We knew all about the effect of marijuana but he didn't, and the total change in his demeanour gave us all a good laugh. The poor innocent didn't realise he was utterly stoned!

But the laughs didn't stop then. The next day it was my duty to take some of the UK artists by minibus back to Shannon, the nearest international airport to Castlebar at the time. Unfortunately, somewhere outside a small town the minibus got a puncture, and I shepherded about a dozen musicians off the bus and into the nearest pub to wait while the puncture was fixed.

As we walked into this tiny rural bar, a young girl was polishing glasses behind the bar counter. I knew by her body language that she immediately spotted people she recognised, especially Ian Dury and Chrissie Hynde, both big stars in Ireland, Britain and elsewhere at the time. She rushed out of the pub probably to tell her mates. I'm sure the presence of several international rock stars was not an everyday occurrence, especially in such a rural location.

In the meantime, the minibus was up and running again, and I asked the entourage to get back on board. I was last to leave the pub, where I could hear the unfortunate girl trying to convince her sceptical mates that Ian and Chrissie had indeed been in this pub only a minute ago. I wonder if they ever believed her? These days she would've taken several selfies to back up her story.

THE TOUR MANAGER?

I recall being in a disused cinema in Limerick in the late 80s for a seminar about the music business and aimed at young musicians. One of several other panellists invited down from Dublin for the occasion was to speak about organising a tour of Ireland. The title of her talk was to be 'Tour Management'. Sadly, she didn't make it in time because she got the wrong train from Dublin and found herself heading to Cork! It took her a while to live that one down, let me tell you!

FULL IRISH ANYONE?

Then there was the George 'Ringo' Byrne breakfast incident in Galway. Once again I was in the (bad) company of Richie Taylor and Jackie Hayden, and one of us (I'm not pointing any fingers!) thought it would be a bit of craic to order breakfast for George to be delivered to his room. George was a man with a healthy appetite who preferred traditional, simple fare. So we took his menu card hanging on the back of his hotel door and ordered muesli, yogurt, honey, smoked kippers and just about anything on the menu we knew he'd hate. In a way, the joke backfired, because when we met George next morning he simply expressed some minor disappointment that the breakfast he received wasn't what he'd ordered. When we eagerly asked him if he sent it back he said, 'Aah, Jaysus, no. I ate it,' before asking us what time the bar-car on the train back to Dublin would open. George was truly unstoppable.

He was also a man who was never shy of sharing his opinion with all and sundry, no matter how offensive somebody might find it or how irrational his opinion might be. One of the best/worst examples of that was him telling people in a pub in the Midlands that the Famine was the best thing that had ever happened in Ireland, as every country needs some way of weeding out the weakest in society. As you can imagine, this wasn't a popular view, and I think he spent the rest of the night sheltering behind a newspaper in the pub's other bar.

THE FONZ

Of course he was only one of many who could trot out a quick quip almost on demand. I was walking down Grafton Street one day with Deke O'Brien, some years after I'd left Scoff Records. Deke had been an impressive performer with a number of acts, most notably Bees Make Honey, Nightbus and Stepaside. He had quite a following, not least because he looked like the character The Fonz, from the American TV sitcom *Happy Days*. I said, 'Deke, how come it never happened for you internationally? He summed it up very succinctly when he replied, 'Well, man, the chemistry was right, but the geography was wrong.' I suppose the underlying lesson in such a perceptive comment is that being in the right place at the right time can be a major component in any artist's success. Nice one, Deke!

HAIRY MEMORIES

I was once at a reception in the Law Library in Dublin when a young woman came up to me and said, 'Are you Johnny Lappin?' I admitted I was indeed, and when she didn't seem to remember me, I reminded her that we'd met before. She peered at me, and said 'You've changed.' 'Have I?' I enquired. 'Yes, you've changed your, eh, hairstyle!' I've been bald all my life, but I just let her keep on digging, as the saying goes!

HITTING THE HIGH NOTES … ON THE ROAD

Bands get up to all sorts of pranks and tricks when they're on the road. This probably stems from the boredom of the constant travel. Here's an account of one such 'story' …..

A very well-known Irish band who I can't name (Hi Joe, Billy, Christy & Alan) toured extensively around Ireland. They liked to return to Dublin after every show which could take up to three hours of driving. The lead singer was prone to falling into a deep sleep with his chin resting on his chest. The other lads once ran gaffer tape around his neck and under his eh.. nether regions. They then stood back and roared his name. His head immediately shot up and ……. Well, you can guess the result. Ouch!!

HITS & WRITS

It was also in the Law Library that I was introduced to the Right Honourable Chief Justice of Ireland, Mr Liam Hamilton. When he said to me, 'What business are you in young man?' I replied, 'I'm in the music business, Your Honour.' He looked at me and said, 'Ahh, the music business, a vineyard for lawyers.' Given that one of the most common statements in the business is, 'Where there's a hit there's a writ', I reckon he knew more about the music business than I would've assumed.

LIFE IS LIKE GOLF

I used the fondness I'd developed for golf under Pop's influence to ease the stress. Golf courses are healthy environments and it can be a very intense game that requires serious concentration balanced with the right degree of relaxation. I found it always worked for me and I could successfully switch off in pleasant surroundings and genial company. I saw a sign once that summed it up. It read something like, *Life is like golf, you just get out of one hole and head straight for another.*

But it was through golf I made some genuinely deep friendships, perhaps none more so than that of the late great singer Joe Dolan.

We were both members of the now-defunct MIGS, the Music Industry Golf Society, and I found Joe to be a very funny, down-to-earth guy. We hit it off straightaway and I spent many hours in his company both on and off the golf course. Joe was a great joke teller and we both played off a 12 handicap. I remember one showbiz golfing holiday we made to Miami in a party of 150. We travelled together, and having to wait for an hour in Atlanta for a connecting flight we ordered two beers in a transit lounge bar.

When our flight was called we started making our way to the plane when we heard somebody calling after us. ''Scuse me, Sir, 'scuse me, Sir'. We turned to find we were being followed by the waitress who'd served us our beers. I asked what her problem was, and she said, 'I'd like you to know that we accept tips here sir'. We hadn't even finished the two beers and had paid the expensive tab. So, I said, 'So you accept tips, do you? ...Well here's a tip. Don't ever drive on the right hand side of the road if you ever come to Ireland.' Joe just cracked up and got so much fun out of that incident he told the story for years.

THE SANDWICH & THE BRICK

I was also playing golf when I saw my first mobile phone. I was playing a round at Woodbrook with Dave and Joe Elliott of Def Leppard, and feeling a bit peckish, we speculated about how we might get a sandwich to eat. Joe took this unwieldy device out of his golf bag, which looked like a brick with a phone connected (compared to the miniscule modern models) and proceeded to phone the clubhouse to enquire if they could deliver sandwiches to us on the 12th tee! I'm sure those early mobile phones will someday feature in museums.

HAIR RAISING STUFF

Shortly after I stopped working with Clannad I was doing some consultancy work for Brian Molloy's Folk Promotions in the Lombard Street building in Dublin. Brian was one of the partners in the recording studios (Westland) which was housed in the same premises, and he was also involved with the immortal Dermot Morgan of RTE's legendary comedy radio series *Scrap Saturday*, a satirical radio show which ran every Saturday morning, and later of *Father Ted* television fame. Dermot Morgan and Gerry Stembridge wrote brilliant scripts for *Scrap Saturday*. The programme ran from 1989 to 1991 and was highly irreverent, poking fun at politicians, authority figures, celebrities and media darlings alike. One of its targets was Donie Cassidy, a Government Senator and prominent showband manager. It was rumoured that Donie wore an expensive hair piece.

In one of the *Scrap Saturday* programmes they referred to Donie as a gobshite, which prompted a very upset Senator to visit Brian in his office. He intimated he wanted an apology, otherwise he couldn't guarantee that Foster and Allen would ever record in Lombard Studios again. I was in Brian's office the day Dermot Morgan called in. Brian politely explained the delicacy of the situation to Dermot in relation to Donie who'd expressed his deep displeasure at being called a gobshite and suggested it might be a good idea to apologise on the following week's programme.

So the following Saturday, I'm driving in my car listening to the *Scrap Saturday* show during which Dermot came on in one of his many guises and said, 'In last week's programme we referred to Senator Donie Cassidy as a gobshite. We'd like to absolutely and unreservedly apologise to Donie and to state that he's NOT a gobshite. He is in fact a complete and utter gobshite. Furthermore, we wish to confirm that his hair is his own because we've seen the receipt!' So Donie got his apology, but maybe not the one he was expecting! And I nearly crashed the car, I was laughing so hard!

RINGO & THE 'STONE'

On another occasion I was influential in arranging for Ronnie Wood of The Rolling Stones and formerly of The Faces, to join the panel for a heat of 'The Bacardi Unplugged' band competition organised by *Hot Press* in the bar of Waterford DIT. The week before the event I bumped into Murty Kavanagh, the roadie who worked with Clannad (no relation to Dave, by the way). I asked him 'What are you doing with yourself these days, Murty?'

He told me he was now employed driving Ron Wood who at that time was living in Kildare, north of Dublin city. He also mentioned Ronnie was about to take delivery of a brand new top-of-the-range Mercedes 500s and he was due to take Ronnie out for a spin down the country in this new motor.

1988 Murty meets Canberra

So I mentioned to Murty I'd be in Waterford the following week (judging the band competition) and if Ronnie fancied a drive down that way he could join us for a few drinks and I joked that maybe he'd serve on the judging panel which included the late George Byrne, then a music journalist with the *Irish Independent*, the late Richie Taylor (*Sunday Press* newspaper) and Jackie Hayden who was in charge of the event for *Hot Press*.

Inviting Ronnie Wood was a complete shot in the dark, but I've always believed if you don't ask, people can't even say no, so we were all amazed when just before the competition started, in walked Murty with Ronnie in tow, much to the complete bemusement of the audience and ourselves.

Can you just imagine the students asking each other in amazement if that could *possibly* be the guy from The Rolling Stones? We, the panel, were trying to keep a totally straight face, and that wasn't easy. Ronnie himself was completely at ease and totally affable, as Jackie briefed him on his judging duties. After the music was finished we all retired with Ronnie to the Tower Hotel in Waterford where he enthralled us with stories about Mick Jagger and Rod Stewart, and other well-known musicians' way into the small hours before Murty took him home.

As he prepared to depart, he was given a warm embrace by George who said to him, 'That's for your work with The Faces, not that shite you're peddling now!' Only George would've risked saying something like that and get away with it! Sadly, most of Ronnie's stories are unrepeatable for reasons of good taste, not to mention libel and slander, but it was a kind of surreal night, and yes, there was drink involved! I met Ronnie several other times after that as we both liked to visit Lillies Bordello a renowned late night club in Dublin. *(Hello Mother!)*

SMOOTH OPERATOR

Murty was one of the true characters in the music business, a real Dub and a man of few words. He drove a large white van for Clannad before either I or Dave became involved with the band. So in a way we inherited him as part of the Clannad family. One day while working in the Clannad office in Bray, Dave answered the phone to find it was Murty calling from France where Clannad were touring. He passed the phone to me to deal with Murty who proceeded to tell me, in his best Dublin drawl, 'There's a bit of a problem, Johnny.'

I said, 'What's the problem, Murty?'

'Eh, Johnny, the van's broken down.'

'What do you mean, broken down?'

'Well, Johnny, it's stopped.'

'Yeah, Murty, but what happened that it stopped?'

'Well I was driving down the motorway when this red light came on.'

'Ok, so what did you do then?'

'Well, Johnny, when I got to the next town ...'

'How far was that, Murty?'

'Eh, about a hundred kilometres, Johnny.'

'You mean you drove the van with a red light for a hundred kilometres?'

'Yeah', he said.

Then, I asked him what the latest situation with the van was.

'Well, Johnny, I found this guy who says he can fix it'

'Ok, so how much will that cost, Murty?'

'I don't know Johnny, but if I had three grand I could really operate!'

I've no idea how Murty thought we'd be able to get three grand to him, even if we had it, or what he meant by 'really operate', but it was out of such situations that strange, almost surreal, stories would emerge. The figure of three grand was a real mystery, given the van by that stage was probably only worth one grand at best! And I've no idea how Murty got himself out of that dilemma, but he did.

THE GLASGOW INN

Murty lived for a time in Dublin's Sheriff Street flats. I was driving around there with him one day when we passed a pub which I think was called the Jet Foil and looked very dilapidated.

I asked him about it and he said, 'Yeah Johnny, that pub is known as the Glasgow Inn.'

'The Glasgow Inn? Why?' I asked.

'Because' he said, 'Every time the broken windows are fixed, the glass goes in! So, we call it The Glasgow Inn.'

That's not just a very good example of Murty's droll wit but a typical slice of irreverent Dublin humour too.

MURTY & THE 'VAN'

Murty also plays a starring role in another story involving Clannad and Van Morrison. Van asked Ciaran Brennan to play double-bass on a record he was recording in Dublin and it was left to me to make sure it went off smoothly. So I asked Murty to call into the office where I told him it was absolutely essential that he collect Ciaran and deliver him to Windmill Lane Studios by

9am the following morning. Given the sometimes wayward behaviour of musicians I stressed that even if he had to stay up all night with Ciaran he had to make sure he got to the studio on time without fail. Since Murty didn't drink and was a very punctual man my worry was more with Ciaran than Murty.

The following morning about 11 o'clock Murty strolled into my office. I asked if he'd managed to get Ciaran to Van on time and he confirmed he had. I asked if he'd talked to Van at all and he said he had. In full-on teeth-extraction mode I asked Murty if Van actually spoke to him?

Murty replied, 'Yeah, Johnny, we had a few words alright'.

Exasperated, I said, 'Well what did he say to you, Murty?'

Murty replied, 'He said, 'Who the fuck are you?' '

I suppose I should've known Van and Murty weren't destined to have one of the great conversations of all time.

AN OFFICER AND A HEARSE

Another particularly surreal story I remember was the time that Clannad were about to film the 'In A Lifetime' video with Bono. We were due to shoot the video in Clannad's home place in Gweedore, Co. Donegal. The video storyboard called for the use of a hearse. So we decided to hire a hearse and, for economic reasons, fill it with all the lighting equipment and drive it up from Dublin through Northern Ireland to Donegal. At that time (circa 1985) there were British Army checkpoints at the border between the North and the South of Ireland.

I was back in the office in Dublin when I got a call from Murty explaining to me that a young British squaddie wasn't going to let the hearse and equipment cross the border as he was somewhat suspicious of the contents i.e. lighting equipment instead of a coffin.

I spent some time trying to explain our situation to the young soldier who eventually passed me on to his commanding officer. I was finally able to persuade this senior officer that our situation was genuine but the bizarre nature of that phone call had all my colleagues in the office falling around the place laughing as you can imagine what it sounded like ….. me trying to explain why we needed him to let us across the border with a hearse full of lighting gear. But with Dave and Bono waiting for the imminent arrival of said hearse, I wasn't laughing at all, at the time!

The video 'In A Lifetime' with Clannad featuring Bono (and that hearse) has subsequently been viewed over 2.3 million times on Youtube.

Some of my most amusing memories and stories come from my many visits to _MIDEM_.

'SMOKE' & MIRRORS?

During the Clannad years I was staying in the Martinez Hotel on the Cannes Croisette (beach) with Dave and one of the band members, because in order to keep within our modest budget we all stayed in one room. We were down in the foyer one evening talking and drinking, but decided to retire to our room for a quiet, eh, smoke.

I reckon there were about 12 of us altogether. But for some reason my attention zeroed in on this one guy who I didn't recognise but who'd been with us in the bar and followed us up to our room. In a drink-fuelled temper I rounded on him. I said, 'I don't know who the fuck you are. Come on, get the fuck out of our room, you asshole.', and I ushered him to the door. Just as he was leaving he turned to me and said, 'I might be many things, but I'm not a fucking asshole.' Unfortunately (for me), the following day I learned he was the President of a very important American independent record label, who was a household name in the music biz. Boy, was I embarrassed!

Fortunately, I did make it up with him and we later became good friends. But it wasn't my finest hour! In fairness, I should add that people in the music industry are usually quite forgiving over such lapses, probably because they've all done and said stupid things at one time or another. It's generally not an industry where grudges are held for too long. It's a relatively tight-knit community, and if you make a serious enemy of somebody word gets around very quickly.

THROUGH FREDDY'S LENSE

Some of the most printable tales concern Freddy Bienstock, the hugely-successful American & legendary music publisher with Carlin Music, probably best known as the man responsible for picking the songs for Elvis Presley's records and films. Freddy, who passed away in 2009, was a very funny guy.

I was walking down the Croisette (again) in Cannes with Dave and Paul McGuinness when Freddy hove into view. With a big grin on his face he came over to us, vigorously shook hands with Paul and said, 'I love MIDEM, Paul. We come every year and lie to one another!'

On another occasion he pointed towards a very rich and famous manager of a world renowned solo artist who seemed to have gained some weight. Everyone in our company knew who the (very rich) manager was. Freddy turned to the company, which included me, and said 'Would you look at the size of ******...... He must be eating the money!'

WHO'S YOUR DADDY?

Another funny one, also involving Dave and Paul, occurred when the three of us were having a cocktail around the pool of the Majestic Hotel.

We were sitting there, shades on *trying* to look cool, when this small bald man came over to our table, and in a typically humorous Jewish accent said, 'You're Paul McGuinness! I met you in New York a few years ago and I told you a funny story and you laughed. And I went home to my family and said to my kids 'Children, Paul McGuinness laughed at Daddy's story', and one of my kids said, 'Who's Daddy?'

NEWBIE NONSENSE

Some of the newcomers to MIDEM would be out to impress by boasting about their contacts or achievements, and this was something Irish delegates were not immune from. One year, this young and inexperienced newbie came into an informal gathering of seasoned MIDEM delegates hanging out at the Martinez Hotel bar.

He started boring the arse off the company with his boasting and name-dropping and talking horse-shite, which as a fellow Irishman, I found embarrassing. Before he made a complete and utter arse of himself I took him aside and explained a couple of realities. However big he thought his achievements were they weren't as big as those of the people he was now trying to impress. Then I told him this, 'Here's some free advice for you, John. You should never miss a good opportunity to shut the fuck up.' That stopped him in his tracks, and I think he took the advice, although he's no longer in the music business.

DANCIN' ON THE CEILINGS

There's a bar in Cannes called La Chunga close by the Martinez Hotel. It's a very lively place, and there's this terrific and very entertaining Spanish guitar player doing his thing. It operates as an after-dinner bar. So the entertainment rarely starts before 11 pm. It has low ceilings and rows of tables around the walls, leaving floor space for dancing. It was a popular spot with beautiful young females as well as patrons who might best be described as 'ladies of negotiable affection', some of who'd be looking for a good time and might be persuaded to dance on the tables, while touching the ceilings, among other things.

By the time it gets to about 2am it begins to resemble the last days of the Roman Empire, with the champagne in full flow. You can imagine the cost of a serious bottle of champagne when a small bottle of beer cost about €12 while shorts will set you back *at least* €18 a pop (without a mixer!).

One year I got a call from the Celtic Woman office telling me our wonderful fiddle player Mairead Nesbitt was in Cannes visiting a friend and if I was free to show her around. Mairead's great company, so I asked if she'd any preference for the evening, would she like to go to a live show, dinner, a bar maybe, or what? She said she'd let me decide but her preference was for something a little different. So I spoke to the man who runs La Chunga, and booked a table where we could observe the madness. Despite the fact Mairead's travelled the world with Celtic Woman and has probably seen most of what the world has to offer, she laughed her head off and was amazed by the wild carry-on to such an extent she still talks about it! If there'd been chandeliers they'd have been swinging out of them. On the way out she admitted she'd asked for something a little different and that's exactly what she got! But don't get the wrong impression, there's nothing sleazy or seedy about the behaviour of the bar's patrons, as the proprietors wouldn't allow any of that! It's just a bit of bonkers fun for those types of night owls. Worth a visit if you're that way inclined!

BEWARE THE BARRACUDAS!

Close to La Chunga in Cannes was a smallish private 'club' called Le Barracuda, very aptly named because it eats your money. It'd be known as a 'hostess' club, and staffed by young ladies who aren't overly dressed and would also do some pole dancing. The French call these types of clubs 'American Bars'.

As soon as you come through the door they're quickly over to offer you a drink. You only discover when you get the bill that a glass of champagne will set you back about €40 and a beer could be €20. The ladies keep a close eye on you so as soon as your glass is nearly empty they very kindly top it up for you. They might even suggest you get an entire bottle of champagne which could cost upwards of €300. If you do buy a bottle several girls come over and they'll all have a glass so your bottle rarely lasts too long and they'll try to persuade you to buy another one. Before you know where you are you've run up a bill of a couple of grand.

In the early days of my first visit to Cannes (1979) it was the custom for delegates to wear ties into such places in the evening. I was most bemused to discover when I first (naively) entered this establishment, when one of the ladies approached me holding a scissors, cut half my tie off and pinned it on the wall. The idea being I'd come back another year and visit it! Beware!

These stories are all part of the madness that was in the early years of Rock'n'Roll ....

Chapter Seventeen

MY MOST MEMORABLE SONGS

Over the years I've often been asked what type of music I, as a professional music publisher like to listen to myself. Given that I have very eclectic music tastes, the problem with answering such a question is that there are always going to be songs you'd like to include but can't. There's the added matter that your attitude to songs can change from time to time, and the list you compile next month will be different from the one you made yesterday. That's the way it is with music.

So for this list I've tried to focus not only on my own personal favourites but also those that had a considerable impact on my personal life and career. There are more than a couple of dozen, but there's no significance to the order I've listed them in.

'Life's Been Good' Joe Walsh (1978)
A great 'tongue in cheek' song about the life of a successful musician.

'She Came In Through The Bathroom Window' The Beatles (1969)
A fine example of a song I love but with words I have never really understood.

'Let's Dance' David Bowie (1983)
The standout track on the first bootleg album I ever bought. (When I learned they were illegal I didn't buy bootlegs any more)

'Only A Woman's Heart' Eleanor McEvoy (1992)

This is not only one great song but the initial version by its composer Eleanor McEvoy and Mary Black kick-started a virtual industry of its own that spawned over a million album sales and several sell-out tours.

'Lives In The Balance' Jackson Browne (1986)

This is a very political song with a strong message by one of my favourite songwriters.

'Losing You' Rob Burke (1994)

A great song I published but, sadly, never had a hit with.

'Many Of Horror (When We Collide)' Biffy Clyro (2009)

To my ears this is a classic rock ballad and proof that heavy rock can also be subtle and gentle at the same time.

'Summer In Dublin' Liam Reilly/Bagatelle (1980)

The mood of a nation was captured in this song. 'Rock'n'roll never forgets' is a terrific line. Liam is a good friend of mine, who I briefly managed.

'Don't Crash The Ambulance' Mark Knopfler (2004)

A wonderful title for a classy song with fine lyrics.

'Pop Muzik' M (1979)

One of those rare occasions when I knew the first time I heard the record it was going to be a monster hit.

'The Island' Paul Brady (1985)

A true classic and arguably the ultimate Irish protest song.

'Pump It Up' Elvis Costello (1978)

Raw energy from a genuine rebel.

'Into The Great Wide Open' Tom Petty (1991)
This song reflects on aspects of the music industry. I love all the late Mr. Petty's work.

'Subterranean Homesick Blues' Bob Dylan (1965)
Bob's a poet for our times, and this song is a classic example of why. I met Mr. Dylan briefly once, an honour.

'Past The Point of Rescue' Mick Hanly (1988)
In my view, one of the best country songs ever written by an Irishman. Check out the production on Hal Ketchum's version.

'Army Dreamers' Kate Bush (1980)
This anti-war song is about a mother grieving for her son who died in action. She feels guilty she might've been able to prevent it. A fine song about life and death.

'Take Me To Church' Hozier (2014)
A unique song that will surely form the foundation of a long creative career.

'Real Real Gone' Van Morrison (1990)
This is Van the Man at his best. He was a real, real inspiration to me when I saw him live in 1964.

'Wish You Were Here' Pink Floyd (1975)
Everybody seems to love the sentiment in Roger Waters' lyric.

'The Last Thing On My Mind' Tom Paxton (1964)
One of my earliest memories of a great song.

'The Kid' Buddy Mondlock (1984)
Expresses in a song, a dream which lots of people have.

'Reelin' and Rockin' Chuck Berry (1958)

This is real a rock'n'roll example from an early master of the art.

'She's Always A Woman' Billy Joel (1977)

A simple, perfect song that encapsulates the essence of those wonderful creatures called women and written by a man who clearly knows his subject!

'One' U2 (1991)

A hugely commercial success, but stylistically quite unlike most other U2 hits.

'Your Song' Elton John (1971)

A song that still stands out, and from one of the pioneers of the singer-songwriter genre.

'Teenage Dirtbag' Wheatus (2000)

A classic American teen band single that's virtually impossible to emulate. This song recently appeared as a sync* for the dating website *Match.com*.

'It's My Life' Bon Jovi (2000)

A realistic, and at the same time inspirational, song about life.

'Crazy World' Aslan (1993)

This is such a great song, and I still can't understand why it's never been a worldwide hit.

'The Next Voice You Hear' Jackson Browne (1997)

I love the sentiment in a song that, for me, contains the perfect lyric ... 'throw down your truth and check your weapons.' Indeed!!

'The Last Resort' Stepaside (1980)

This song was written by the band's late bassist Paul Ashford. I particularly like the version with Ronnie Drew (Dubliners) speaking the words which are Paul's reflections on his home town of Bray where he was reared. It's on

Stepaside's album *Sit Down and Relapse*. Check it out on Youtube, 'cause it's worth it!

'Human' Rag'n'Bone Man (2017)
First time I heard this song it stopped me in my tracks. A huge hit all over the world (except America, for some strange reason which also puzzles Elton John!)

'These Days' Jackson Browne (1973)
Says it all really.....

'Don't Give Up' Peter Gabriel (featuring Kate Bush) (1986)
A perfect collaboration. Such an inspiring song. Timeless.

'Cry Me A River' Justin Timberlake (2002)
271,167,621 people liked this song (Youtube) so I'm in good company.

'This Is America' Childish Gambino (2018)
Sadly, this *is* America these days.

I could go on, and on, adding songs to this list forever. One of these days I'll get around to making one of those Spotify playlists and all of the above will definitely feature. But 'Time(s) the Conqueror', as Jackson Browne once wrote....

Chapter Eighteen

HEROES AND VILLAINS

The Heroes

There are many reasons for admiring people in music, and some of them, obviously, relate to the music itself and the creativity they bring to it. But I also admire smart musicians who, instead of taking on the role of helpless victims as many do; they take control of their own music and careers. I admire anyone who can make a living from the expression and dissemination of their art.

Being a successful artist in any arts discipline is a difficult task in itself, so to be able to make a living from it is even more worthy of admiration.

In that regard, the late **David Bowie** immediately comes to mind. He effectively sold shares in himself in 1997 using his 25 albums as a kind of collateral. These were known as Bowie Bonds. Bowie sacrificed ten years of future royalty income in return for an advance payment of $55 million. Whether this was a winning investment for others I can't say, but it certainly gave Bowie a fast and considerable return which he used to buy up the copyrights in his own songs.

Paul Simon is another songwriter who owns his own publishing now and he's not the only one. I know some people baulk at the idea of a creative artiste soiling his hands with filthy lucre, but they seem unaware that geniuses of the stature of Beethoven, Shakespeare, Wagner, Dickens and Picasso, among other greats, had no problem making sure they got a satisfactory return for their creativity. If that policy was good enough for Shakespeare it can't do much harm to Paddy Songwriter.

I have much to be thankful for in the generous help and advice I've received over the years from my good friend and fellow music publisher, **Nigel Elderton**. Currently Nigel is the Chairman of the Performing Rights Society *(PRS)* in the UK. In his day job he's President of the UK and Europe with the global music publishing giants Peermusic, and has regularly given me the benefit of his vast knowledge of the intricate digital rights segment of our business and I've used much of his wisdom when negotiating deals on behalf of my clients. And I'm still learning from him!

Likewise, I know I can also always count on **Stuart Hornall**, another great friend and fellow publisher who controls a number of valuable copyrights through his company Hornall Bros Music, whose strap line is 'Proper Songs' … and indeed they are. One of his clients is Mark Knopfler of Dire Straits fame. Stuart is originally from Scotland (we all have our hard luck stories Stu!) and handles the publishing affairs for Irish acts such as Paul Brady, Chris de Burgh and Eleanor McEvoy.

On the home front I greatly admire **Moya Brennan** of Clannad. She always strikes me as a woman with a beautiful soul, as well as being a true professional. Her gentle but firm diplomacy was much to the fore in Clannad given that the main line-up was made up of her two brothers and two uncles, all male.

Family bands aren't always as free from internal strife as we might assume. The history of rock music offers many examples of sibling rivalry. Phil and Don of The Everly Brothers were at loggerheads for years, and The Beach Boys, despite being built around the three Wilson brothers were like a musical war zone, especially when they were managed by their violent authoritarian father Murry. The rivalry between the Kinks brothers Ray and Dave Davies often spilled over into physical violence and serious verbal abuse. I'm not sure if they even speak to each other these days.

Of course, the internal dynamics of Clannad never descended into anything on that scale, but it was comforting for us on the management side to know that Moya was always there to lend her good sense and soothing voice to smooth things over.

Bono is another Irishman who really inspires me. He doesn't actually have to bother spending any time or make any effort to help the poor and starving people of the world, but he chooses to do it and more luck to him. Whenever he gets a lot of stick for his actions, I'm reminded of that joke about the Irishman with amnesia, 'He forgot everything except the grudge'.

At some point in recent years, U2 donated €5 million to the Irish government for use in the Music Generation project which enables young musicians to have access to musical instruments and general music advice. Apart from Paul McCartney donating £1 million to the Liverpool Institute of Performing Arts I'm not aware of any other acts who've been so generous and so encouraging of Irish talent. I admire the fact that if Bono, or any other member of U2, wants to go to a gig, they generally do so in the company of their mates, whereas a star like Maria Carey or Kanye West would probably need a posse of 20 or 30 before they'd even step onto the street. Irish people and, I'm delighted to say, most Irish artists, don't have much tolerance for that level of pretentiousness.

Of course, U2 have their detractors, but I'm glad to see they pay no attention whatsoever to the whiners, whingers and begrudgers in our midst. I can only assume that such antagonism is driven by small mindedness and envy.

Their recently-retired long-term manager **Paul McGuinness** is another industry insider I admire and respect. He's brought off some incredibly smart and lucrative deals for his clients that include excluding the compilation rights from U2 record deals. This meant that no company could release a greatest hits package of the band's material without negotiating a fresh deal with the band. While the band signed to CBS Records in Ireland, they signed to Island Records, owned by Chris Blackwell, for the rest of the world. It got to a point, according to music industry folklore, that the label owed U2 a vast sum of money in lieu of royalties. Unfortunately, due to cash flow problems, Blackwell didn't have the wherewithal to meet the royalty debt. And as he was in the process of negotiating the sale of the label to the major Polydor Records, he offered to give U2 a percentage ownership of Island Records in lieu of those royalties. It's believed this deal netted U2 something in the region of

£30 million (and that's sterling, folks!). Not a bad day's work at all.

Another towering figure in the Irish music industry, and a man who's made a ginormous impression all across the globe, is **Bob Geldof**. He transformed the Irish rock music landscape, partly through the frenetic nature of the music he created with the Boomtown Rats, but also with his in-your-face personality. He went on the *Late Late Show* and shocked one half of the nation and delighted the rest of us by saying everything about Ireland we thought but hadn't gotten around to expressing. Geldof did that for us and let that genie out of the bottle. He didn't so much break the rules as ignore them. When 'The Rats' played support to Tom Petty and the Heartbreakers at the Rainbow Theatre in London, they hung up banners outside the nearest tube station that read, 'Rats Eat Heartbreakers For Breakfast'. Typical Geldof, and a sign of things to come.

Van Morrison is another artist I admire, not just for the quality of his work but also his determination to follow his own musical instinct. While in London in 2014 for the BMI Awards I met him and took the opportunity to tell him I'd played support to him at the Stella House in Dublin (circa 1964). I'd stood at the side of that stage as he performed 'Gloria' with his band called Them. As a result, I learned the words of 'Gloria' and added it to our repertoire.

When I told him this he looked and me and asked, 'Are you a musician?'

I said, 'I was a musician then.'

'Are you a musician now?'

'No, I'm a publisher now.'

'What's your name?'

'My name is Johnny Lappin.'

'Johnny Lappin? I've heard of you.'

I walked away thinking. 'Wow, Van Morrison's heard of me? Fame at last!'

Last but not least, I have a huge amount of time and respect for the Road Crew community, or **Mother Truckers** as they're affectionately known in the industry. These are the people who effectively keep the show on the road. They're generally a dedicated bunch of highly specialised technicians, including sound engineers, lighting designers and operators, guitar and 'backline' techs and so on. They're the backbone and often the unsung heroes of the live performance circuit!

They say you should never meet your heroes. I have one memory of just such an occasion albeit this is a happy one ....

When I was getting into music in the late 1960's and early 1970s, one of the musicians I really admired was the American singer/songwriter **Kris Kristofferson**. His song 'Sunday Mornin' Comin' Down' (later to be a 1983 hit for Johnny Cash), was one of my favourites not least because I was vaguely familiar with the songs sentiments! I also loved his tongue in cheek track, 'Jesus was a Capricorn' (1972).

Sometime in the 2000s Kris was doing a gig in Dublin's Olympia Theatre and as it was an MCD promotion I had a ticket to the show and the after party. So, I got to meet Kris backstage at the bar and at one point I said to him, 'You know what Kris? You were one of the reasons I got into music in the first place.' He looked at me and said in his slow Texan drawl, 'Hey, Johnny, don't pin that one on me, man'.

We had a lot of fun that night and it's a memory I treasure and will never forget.

The Villains

Like every other business, the music industry has spawned its own share of villains, people whose behavior inevitably gives any industry a bad name. **Colonel Tom Parker** did much for the career of Elvis Presley but was also a charlatan and a crook. He had the possibly legal but definitely immoral policy of often insisting to songwriters who submitted songs for Presley's consideration, that Elvis must be credited with 50% songwriter royalties for songs he'd record but had no part whatsoever in writing. Many of these songs ended up as B sides on Elvis singles, because Parker realized that the mechanical royalties for A sides and B sides were split equally, so a hit single could earn substantial royalties for the B side's writer.

Many of Parker's business decisions seemed to have been driven by his own greed for money and not to the best advantage of the artist whose career he was supposed to be managing. He arranged for Elvis to act in some films that were spectacularly awful and often made more money from Presley projects than Elvis did. Elvis lost vast sums of money because he never toured abroad. Parker came up with spurious excuses for this, but it's generally suspected he was an illegal alien and mightn't have been able to get the necessary passport. He wasn't a colonel either, and although he claimed to be born in West Virginia, he was really Andreas Van Kuijk from Holland.

Another undesirable individual was **Murry Wilson**, a man who wasn't only a vicious violent Father but who cheated his own sons out of millions! He was the father of Beach Boys, Brian, Carl and Dennis Wilson, and without consulting them, famously sold their wonderful catalogue of songs for $750,000, a pittance compared to the $20 million valuation put on it by industry insiders at the time. It was said that as an aspiring songwriter himself he was deeply jealous of his sons' success, especially Brian.

The Englishman **Don Arden** managed such major acts as the Small Faces, ELO and Black Sabbath. He cultivated an image of an aggressive businessman who'd use threats of violence, outrageous lies and other dodgy scams to trick his artists out of money. He was so nasty that even his own family, including his daughter Sharon Osbourne, cut off all contact with him. She later told an interviewer, 'He taught me everything not to do. My Father's never even seen any of my three kids and, as far as I'm concerned, he never will.' Villains don't come much worse.

Many of the problems that beset the industry in the past have been eliminated in more recent times, partly because many artists are more astute regarding their business dealings and engage legal experts, who know the music industry, and work on their behalf. But as we've seen with the corruption in banking and other industries worldwide, when there's a pile of money to be scammed from the vulnerable and the unwary, there's always a villain ready to try it on.

Eagle-eyed readers will see that the Villains referred to above are all dead! For obvious reasons, I'm not naming any living Villains! I'll leave an additional Chapter in my Will, which Colette will have published just before she leaves the country! LOL

Chapter Nineteen

THE INTERNET AND THE CHALLENGES AHEAD

The first genre of musicians who seemed to understand the impact of the Internet were indie rock musicians. They were generally young, savvy, and knew their way around it because of their intimate knowledge of computer technology. Then they went a bit crazy. Some saw the web as the final blow in the demolition of the major record labels they despised and hurried to embrace the new technology like lovelorn early teens.

They soon came up with a winning plan which went as follows:

Bands would give their music away free via the net, which in turn would help them build a fan-base, which would then get them gigs at which they could sell loads of hard-copy CDs, as well as their t-shirts, posters, baseball hats or any other merchandise they had, perhaps even including fridge magnets with their logo emblazoned thereon. Some critics actually used to refer cynically to this as the 'fridge magnet plan'.

The big flaw in this was there weren't enough gigs or people prepared to attend them. Equally, venue promoters quickly learned that under this plan bands would be even more dependent on gigs, so they could play one band off against ten others, to the advantage of nobody, apart from the promoter.

Then, ironically, among the first casualties in music from the rise of the Internet were indie record labels who previously could survive selling maybe 20,000 copies of a CD, but who now found sales in freefall towards zero. Most of them went out of business as they had no other means of income.

'Music is free', became a catchphrase for many, but none of them explained why music should be free and not bread, potatoes, turnips, books or even vodka. In the real world, music is a commodity and somebody has to make it the way consumers want to receive it. I've no problem when someone wants to give away their own music for free, but have little truck with those who want to steal income from the artists they claim to be fans of. To me, they're not fans, just thieves.

Of course, the record companies initially had the absurd idea that if they ignored the Internet, or treated it like some tiresome passing fad, it would simply go away. They adopted that head-in-the-sand attitude with the arrival of Sean Fanning and Napster in 1992, with its facility to enable music thieves to share music files for free. The record companies looked away, hoping the threat would pass, and when it didn't and the situation worsened they had to buy Napster for a pile of money. But by then it was too late. They'd lost the battle, and came close to losing the war.

Like nearly all inventions, the Internet brings advantages and disadvantages. Initially it was referred to as 'the information super-highway' and it's made an extraordinary amount of information available to us at our fingertips. You can track down advice on all manner of subjects, usually for free, a major change from my early days when you often had to learn from trial and error, mostly error. But claims that the Internet was going to destroy music have proved to be unfounded. In fact, we've been here before, and often. We've been told the availability of films on videos would close cinemas, 24-hour television news channels would force newspapers to fold and pay-per-view concerts on our screens would kill live music. Etc.

The doomsayers have been wrong time after time. Sure, all of these inventions have changed the landscape, but smart people accept them and adapt, often because they've no choice and it's virtually impossible to hold back progress. Once something's been invented, it's not going to be un-invented.

It's helped get rid of many of the excesses of the sixties and seventies when bands and their entourages seemed to compete to see who could behave most badly.

Keith Moon of The Who throwing televisions out of hotel windows was very funny and we all laughed, unless you were in danger of stopping one before it hit the ground. For a while, stars behaved as outrageously as fans and the media expected. This was dealt with, in part, by record companies and management making bands pay for their excesses, and that curbed much of the silliness, although it probably led to a reduction in tales to tell the grand-children. But it also led to many claiming that a lot of the madcap mayhem and colour has gone out of the music scene.

The Internet and the proliferation of social media have enabled an act to turn itself into a sort of cottage industry in which that act can take greater control of its recordings, marketing, career path and income streams. But in order for that act to thrive, or even survive, they have to take on a heavy workload, and that work has to be taken seriously, and they have to learn to move with the changes and roll with the punches.

Yes, musicians have a lot more freedom getting music out there and that's a good thing in an artistic sense, but it also means the level of choice for fans is overwhelming. I heard of a *Grateful Dead* website with over 12,000 live concerts available for free. Assuming their concerts might, on average, be three hours long, almost certainly a serious under-estimation, I whiled away some time calculating how long it would take me to listen to them all just once if I made it my full-time 9-to-5 job. It'd take more than a decade! And that's just one artist with career longevity.

The amount of music, both live and recorded, that's now available online is overwhelming, and the marketplace is further cluttered by families uploading 8-year-old Jenny singing 'My Way' at her brother's wedding. They're perfectly entitled to do this, but all of it adds to the clutter. And fans, as well as artists, react equally to ongoing changes as they come down the track. Only a few years ago the main industry message proclaimed that the future was in downloading. But it didn't take long before that turned out to be a false dawn, as downloading was soon overshadowed by streaming. This led to the intense competition we now see between Spotify and its rivals, including Apple, Tidal and Deezer. Who knows who'll win what could be a race to the bottom.

In the meantime, the Irish music industry struggles to understand why there's no Irish playlist submitted from Ireland to Spotify. For reasons no one seems able to explain, Irish recordings come under the jurisdiction of a Music Editor based in London. So there's another lobbying battle to be fought on that front in order to get that anomaly fixed.

Another battle being undertaken by music publishers is to bring their songwriters income from companies such as Spotify in line with the revenue from the same recordings that go to the record companies. But guess who the majority share-holders are in Spotify? … Yep, Sony, Universal, and Warner Bros.

While YouTube was initially seen as the enemy, the industry learned from its mistakes over Napster and decided to work with it. So the situation has improved over what it was a few years back. And while virtually anybody can now upload a video performance on YouTube, Twitter or Facebook, how do you efficiently monetise your investment or market it to the world? So I really feel we're still at the frontier. Remember, Apple only launched their iTunes store in 2003!

And there have been many other changes, with retailers especially paying a heavy price, and not just in music. Many people, very unfairly in my view, use the local clothes shop to try on new items, and, having found something they like, go home and order it online at a cheaper price. We've seen the impact on the travel business with the disappearance of agencies from high streets all over the world. Now it's almost all done online. The book business has also suffered, with many bookshops also closing. Online piracy of new films, where the investment is vastly higher than in recording music, is making it less profitable for film companies to make big budget blockbuster movies.

The drop in CD sales has resulted in the disappearance of record shops as we knew them. And it's not just in Ireland, but worldwide. Now, apart from a few plucky independent-minded survivors, you'll be more likely to find a small number of CDs for sale in your local supermarket or computer store. In Ireland we had five or six sizeable record distributors with substantial warehouses, they're nearly all gone now, and even the Irish wing of the major record companies mostly distribute their records from UK bases.

That shrinking in the retail area is one of the reasons why most artists who still make physical CDs have turned to selling them at live shows. And while there might be less online music piracy, if musicians and record companies can't expect a reasonable return on their investment, fewer people will make music. In Ireland we've recently seen Aslan, one of our most popular pop-rock bands, publicly admit they can't afford to fund a new album because they received so little return from the online use, much of it illegal, of their last effort, despite its considerable popularity.

I'd love to come back in fifty years to see how it all eventually shapes up. It's also interesting to note that many new artists often disregard radio stations of the traditional variety because they can get their music out to the world via YouTube, Spotify, Soundcloud and numerous other channels, and music fans now have thousands of radio stations to choose from, so the level of radio play for (Irish) artists may be far less critical for some of them than it would've been in the pre-digital era.

Then there's the speed at which new material can be released. An artist can make a new recording this morning and have it available worldwide this afternoon, whereas under the old vinyl or CD processes it could take weeks to get it to the fans, and maybe longer, especially if the manufacturing plant was busy or the release had to be slotted into a record company's schedule. Even then it mightn't have been made available in some countries for months, or maybe ever.

The unexpected resurgence of vinyl is yet another reminder of how totally unpredictable this business can be. I'm of an age that grew up with vinyl, and when I listen to a vinyl recording, by, say, Hozier, I feel I'm somehow hearing more of the music than I get through any other medium. But as a serious music fan I welcome all methods of enjoying music so individual fans can make their own choices, and I take heart from the fact that young fans are buying vinyl too.

Today, an artist can certainly make an impact exclusively via the Internet, great fun and very rewarding in its own right, but it doesn't automatically translate into anything much beyond that. You can build up staggering numbers of hits with your YouTube video, but that doesn't mean many will go to see you live, or stream or download your music in a way that constitutes a real career. And while the current focus is on streaming, who knows how that might change in the months/years ahead? And that's precisely why I find the music business so exciting and constantly challenging.

Of course, the Internet hasn't made it any easier to persuade people to part with their money, and the endless options for the consumer have reinforced the competitive nature of the business side of music. But these are comparatively early days, and I believe most of us are only beginning to explore the new possibilities in terms of marketing and distribution.

Overall, and on mature reflection, I don't think music publishers were as naive as record companies when the Internet arrived, and as a music publisher I quickly learned to embrace the Internet. Nor have I any strong feelings as to the means through which music can be disseminated. They can embed music on beer mats or in sugar cubes, I don't care so long as those who own the rights to it give their permission and are properly remunerated.

And the Internet has added to the complexities of Music Publishing too. It's expanding and developing at such a speed that the various legal and justice systems in most countries struggle to keep up. We've always needed a working knowledge of copyright laws as they vary from country to country, but we also contend with the fact that some countries, such as Russia, North Korea, Iran, Iraq and China, have a zero-to-lukewarm attitude to copyright anyway.

Added to that, while the global industry strives to move in the direction of harmonisation right across the board, the USA seems to be moving towards a period of isolationism which doesn't sit too well with those aspirations. By virtue of their size, the music markets in Russia, China and India have enormous earning potential for music publishers if changes can be made to their copyright laws, so there may be some light ahead. The decision by the Indian government to give away free smartphones to college students, plantation workers, farmers, and labourers, is one very positive move in our favour.

I'm also aware that virtually all the key Internet players whose work affects the music industry are American, including Google, Facebook, Apple, YouTube, Twitter and Amazon, thereby giving that country an enormous dominance over the global industry. I don't know where we'd turn if one day Google announces it'll no longer provide a free service and we're suddenly into a pay-up-or-else scenario.

If that sounds fanciful, just bear in mind that Facebook has started a pilot scheme enabling Facebook group administrators to charge people who want to join certain groups. Furthermore, YouTube has already given details of their Music Premium service, the new subscription tier for Google's video service that's already available in the UK, Germany, France, Spain, Italy, Russia, Canada, Ireland, the US and Australia. Am I just an old cynic, or do I foresee a time in the near future when YouTube will be only available to those who pay?...I'm just saying, is all.

One way or the other, the short-lived argument that all music should be free has more or less disappeared, although I accept that musicians and songwriters have the right to give away their *own* music for free if they choose. Pirate sites are generally being closed down as soon as they open.

Meantime, the music business has been at loggerheads with YouTube among others, arguing that while viewers watching music videos via its platform generate ad revenue for YouTube, little of this goes to the artists, songwriters, music publishers or record labels who invest talent, time and resources into the business.

Under current legislation, media platforms haven't been held responsible for overseeing the legality of a particular piece of content until it was brought to their attention. It's as if it would be ok for me to steal your car, as long as I give it back to you, if you ask me to! But proposed new copyright rules, under consideration by the European Parliament in 2018, will require platforms such as YouTube to actively prevent copyrighted material from being used without a license from the copyright owners. They'll also give more power to rights holders to demand compensation for the use of their material. Furthermore, if these proposals become law, YouTube could owe billions in back payments for any unlicensed material it may have used in the past.

We also have Apple showing an interest in the Music Publishing market, so keeping track of the varying ways in which copyright music can be transmitted across the Internet, as well as the money it generates, adds to the complexity of the situation for those involved at an international level, and that's likely to increase.

Music is also now being composed by AI (artificial intelligence), so who knows what impact that might have on the music industry at several levels. In a sense, the only constant in Music Publishing is change, and the business motto has to be 'adapt or die', but the future should be less bleak all round if and when legislation globally begins to really catch up with current technologies. In that regard, it's encouraging to note the Americans are talking about the modernisation of their copyright laws. It's quite clear to me that most copyright laws everywhere are sadly no longer fit for purpose, and that applies as much in Ireland as it does around the world, from the USA to China. Although we are in the digital age, we are still being governed by analog laws.

Much is being done by the collection agencies and various consortia to plug the many loopholes in the laws around the globe. In truth, we're still in the wild west of the digital era, and while there's no shortage of outlaws, we'll certainly need a lot more sheriffs.

Chapter Twenty

THE HOZIER STORY - TAKE ME TO THE CHARTS

Perhaps it's now finally time to take up the rest of the Hozier story with which I opened this tome. The value of having built positive personal relationships over the years with key figures in the international music publishing business, especially through attending MIDEM, really came home to me when it came time to negotiate on an international level following the interest generated regarding Hozier's songs. For example, it was at MIDEM that I first met Phil Graham, the number two man at BMI (Broadcast Music Inc) who represent more than 10 million musical works by more than 700,000 songwriters and music publishers in the USA and Canada. We'd met regularly in Cannes, so when it came time to think about a Hozier deal back in 2013 it helped that he knew who I was and that he'd take my call. It underscores the point I made earlier about how MIDEM is not about the deals you do there, but the contacts you make and develop over time, and the access that gives you to the top movers and shakers in the global music industry.

Over the years, since my Scoff and Clannad days, I made dozens of trips to both London and New York City on behalf of various bands, artists and song-writer clients. As a result, I built up a substantial list of heavyweight contacts in the music publishing business. Part of my brief for Evolving was to score an international sub publishing deal for the catalogue, and I felt I was making progress, albeit slowly. However, I couldn't help noticing when the initial frenzy started around 'Take Me To Church' that interest in the catalogue perked up, not least because it now included such a hot and happening artist/songwriter as Hozier.

But while the interest brought its own satisfaction it also came with a heavy workload. I was constantly in receipt of a variety of contract offers from overseas. Some were amendments to previous offers, but each different in its own right and each had to be evaluated on its own merits. This required much detailed and concentrated reading and study, not to mention endless emails and phone calls, and I was enormously conscious this was something I'd only get one shot at. If I went for the wrong deal, there'd be no second chances and no turning back. I knew this was a shot at the big time, as they quaintly call it. I had full confidence and belief in the talent and calibre of the writers I was representing, and that I had enough experience to maximise a deal on their behalf.

By this point, in 2013, Evolving Music represented an impressive mix of Irish and international songwriters, all of whom were impacting on the global music scene in one way or another. It included Rodrigo y Gabriella, the acoustic instrumental rock duo from Mexico who, with 5 studio albums and 3 live albums, had generated sales of nearly 2 million. We had the acclaimed Dublin rock trio Original Rude Boys whose 'Never Gonna Walk Away' won 'Song of The Year' at the Meteor Choice Music Awards in 2014 and who extended their fan base when they toured Europe and Australia with The Script. Also, from Dublin were the increasingly popular power-pop trio The Minutes. Their song 'Black Keys' was used by Carlsberg for the Euro 2012 football championships and also featured on the soundtrack of the sci-fi horror film *Grabbers*.

Another Irish act signed to Evolving Music was the alternative rock quartet Funeral Suits. Their disturbing, if intriguing, video for their song 'All Those Friendly People' had racked up about 6 million online views alone. Then, Ryan Sheridan's song 'The Dreamer' was used for a Heineken television commercial and his song 'Home' was extensively used in the UK chart-topping film *Mrs Brown's Boys: D'Movie*. Ryan also established himself as an artist of note in several European countries, including Germany. John Murry, from California, his debut album *The Graceless Age* had attracted glowing reviews in such prestigious publications as *The Guardian, Q, Mojo, Uncut, The Times* and *The Sun*. The Evolving line-up at that time was completed by the Slovakian classical crossover violinist Vladimir who has already drawn comparisons to the hugely-successful Andre Rieu.

Given that all of these artists were doing fine while signed to Evolving Music in Ireland you might wonder why there'd be a need to assign their songs to a bigger company for the rest of the world outside Ireland? The explanation is one of pure pragmatism and logistics. Linking up with a company that has a presence in such key markets as the USA, Canada, Australia, Japan and the UK, as well as key European countries and elsewhere opens up opportunities for songwriters that would be so much harder to take advantage of through a small office in Dublin. So I knew my client's interests would best be served if I could negotiate a major worldwide deal for the entire Evolving Music catalogue and not just one of our songwriters. Without doubt, that approach gave me more bargaining power, so I encouraged all interested global publishing companies to think in terms of signing the entire catalogue as I was convinced that would be to the benefit of all our artists.

The entire process was fascinating for me on another level. While I'd been involved at the early stages of both Clannad and Celtic Woman and was part of their development as global artists of considerable importance, through the rise of Hozier this was the first time for me to observe at close quarters the development of a new artist born of the digital age. Watching his success was to enlighten me as to how the global music industry had been turned on its head in the internet age and so crucially different from the industry I'd been part of back in the Scoff Records and Clannad days.

Of course, Hozier's unique talent and his artistic maturity, especially given that he was only 23 when he released his fateful first EP, were central to his ability to scale the heights of the music world. His real name is Andrew Byrne and he hails from Newcastle in County Wicklow not far from the town of Bray where Dave and I had located our first Clannad offices. The son of liberal-minded parents, he taught himself to play guitar. He attended St Gerard's School in Bray where he was known to Storm, daughter of Caroline and Denis Desmond.

One of Caroline's closest music industry friends is Louis Walsh and when Caroline arranged a fundraising talent competition in aid of St Gerard's, under the name 'The G-Factor', she persuaded Louis to serve as a judge. Hozier, then probably about 17, duly won the competition. It's interesting that while many Irish musicians can be more than a bit sniffy about talent competitions, winning them has hardly impaired the careers of U2, Clannad or, as we shall see, Hozier himself.

A development record deal was then agreed with Universal Music in Ireland, with Louis Walsh suggesting songs for Hozier to record. But these were pop songs that might've been appropriate for the kind of act Louis managed but didn't quite fit in with Hozier's own artistic inclinations. By this time, he was writing his own songs anyway, and in due course we signed him to a publishing deal with The Evolving Music Company Ltd in 2010.

From 2007 to 2012 he'd toured and recorded with the choral ensemble called Anuna and was also a member of the orchestra at Trinity College in Dublin where he'd studied for a time. So, Hozier's talent and commitment to his art were becoming increasingly obvious when he made his first demo. It included some of the songs which appeared on his first EP, such as the eponymous 'Take Me To Church' that had so quickly generated international attention from both fans and the worldwide music industry.

I think I only fully realized the significance of Hozier as a major music talent when I got an advance copy of his self-titled debut album and immediately recognized the consistently high quality of the songs, the depth of his lyrical ability and the range of expression in his distinctive voice.

While attending his second ever gig at the Button Factory in Dublin in October 2013, I was struck by the strength and standard of his songs, while also recognizing he was quite nervous, understandable given the mounting pressure gathering around him.

One of the skills you hope to have picked up over the decades as a publisher is the ability to witness a performance that mightn't be first class in itself, but be able to see under the skin of that performance and evaluate the talent that underpins it. In that regard an experienced insider should be able to see more than the average fan can see, although none of us are infallible.

There's a significant difference between hearing a piece of music in a general and relatively passive way, and actively listening to it in all its details.

After that tentative gig I spoke with Andrew and his band in The Workman's Club beside The Clarence Hotel, and found him to be a particularly engaging young man who, despite his obvious talent, had an endearing humility about him.

2014 Johnny and Hozier at the Olympia, Dublin

So, I was becoming increasingly confident that Hozier could become the latest in a long line of Irish artists to make it internationally. Even with a population of only 4.5 million, our long list of successes is not lost on the top decision-makers in the global music business, including those I would subsequently negotiate with. The line of Irish successes includes U2, The Cranberries, Celtic Woman, Clannad, Thin Lizzy, Van Morrison, Rory Gallagher, The Script, The Chieftains, Chris de Burgh, Val Doonican, Sinead O'Connor, Boyzone, Boomtown Rats, Westlife and many others, not to mention our terrific track record in the Eurovision Song Contest.

That's an impressive list by any standard. But I suspect those global successes have been spurred by the fact that it's virtually impossible for such acts to make a living from Ireland alone, so they're forced to turn their attention beyond Ireland, even if it means, as in the case of U2, spending a long time touring the USA in a transit van before the big time finally beckons.

It also helps that much of the Irish music industry and the music media is accessible to acts in Ireland to an extent it might not be elsewhere, and that creates a sense of Ireland as a fine nursery where artists can learn more about the industry and how the music media works. We're also a very garrulous nation with a fine grasp of the English language, and I've heard it said by media professionals in the UK that even though they might not have cared much for Boyzone's music as such, they were always more relaxed and more fun to have in a TV or radio studio, compared to a less experienced, less talkative act from a small UK town or village.

So, it was exciting for me to be in at the start of another new Irish phenomenon setting off to conquer the musical world when back in October 2013 a frenzy of attention saw a succession of major, and some not-quite-so-major international music publishers eagerly bidding for the Evolving Music catalogue that included Hozier.

My first decision, apart from telling myself to stay cool and not to panic, was to find a good lawyer I could work with and one who understood the intricacies of contracts at their most complex and the possible implications of every word proposed in them. A misunderstood phrase can lose you millions of dollars, and might only consist of three small words in a document of 100 pages long, written in the kind of arcane language that only legal eagles seem to understand. This isn't something you can do on the cheap or hand over to your friendly neighbourhood solicitor who may be adept at house conveyance but knows little about the music business. I've seen far too many people make those mistakes over the years to fall into that trap myself.

I remembered a London based young lawyer called Sebastian Davey, who I'd been highly impressed with when he was representing a songwriter that I was once looking to sign to Evolving. In effect, Sebastian was on the other side of the table during those negotiations, and I now wanted the opportunity to have him on my side and have my clients benefit from the legal expertise he'd clearly shown back then, as well as his deep understanding of the music industry.

I'd already sent out a generic e-mail letter to all the music publishing companies who'd shown genuine interest in doing business with Hozier, and in it I outlined the strength of the Evolving catalogue and brief details of the company's history and background. I also indicated what kind of deal I was happy to talk about.

As matters developed I reckoned there were eight companies who were serious contenders, including virtually all of the major companies and some others of considerable significance.

I arranged to meet all 8 over a three-day period in London in November 2013. Before each meeting I used my contacts to find out as much as I could as to how each of these companies operated. This was a bit daunting, as I was handling these preliminary meetings on my own with a view to ascertaining in general terms what kind of deal each one might offer.

I also found myself walking into some unexpected situations. In one instance I went into a meeting that was scheduled with one person only to find the heads of nine different departments within that company arranged around a large boardroom table. They may have hoped that such a show of force would intimidate me, but if they did they got that wrong. Being a stickler for attention to detail, I'd done my research on the company and knew who all the various department heads were.

Another company brought me in and showed me a map of the world, with all their offices marked on it, while different members of their team boasted about their wonderful internal systems. It didn't take me long to realise that I'd probably carried out more research on them than they had on me, and some of them might've assumed that since I *merely* represented an Irish publishing company I might be green in more ways than one. If they did think that way, they got that wrong too.

On the other hand, there was one company I went to meet, and I immediately felt at ease in what was an old rock'n'roll-style office. I learned that the head of the company had his office on the same floor as the A&R people, as opposed to being upstairs alongside the business affairs department as is often the case. I was encouraged by the fact that the top man felt the need to be close to those who dealt with the company's talent and prospective signings. Overall it was a revelation to see the different approaches of the various companies I met.

While I was engaged in this round of negotiations there was a separate and parallel race being run by the record companies to sign Hozier, and I was aware that an artist who has a record deal is more attractive to a music publishing company than one who hasn't. So, it suited my strategy to allow the record company deal to work itself out before I concluded a publishing deal.

The stakes were increasing as time went by. It's not unlike playing poker and having a good poker face. Of course, while the potential financial income from a contract is a serious factor in going with one offer over another, there are other factors that need to be considered. I was conscious that since this was going to be a long-term project I needed to feel comfortable with the team I'd be dealing with on a long-term basis. I wanted to have a sense that I could trust their understanding of what Evolving, and its roster of artists were about, and to feel convinced that they were committed to maximising the potential of all the songwriters who formed part of that roster both at that time and in the future.

Fortunately, 40 years' experience has given me a reasonably good instinct for sussing who's on top of their game and who's struggling. By now I reckoned I should be able to spot waffle at a hundred paces! During the many conversations I had during these prolonged negotiations I'd often fire out a question about an artist in our Evolving catalogue just to see if they responded with any real knowledge or were just winging it.

Another skill essential for scoring the best deal is to recognise one when it shows up. Here again, I've seen countless deals screwed up by inexperienced managers and artists who worked on the assumption that whatever deal is on the table this week will be superseded by a better deal next week. Yes, that can happen, but it can also result in the shocking discovery that the company who made that offer last week haven't been back to you at all this week and, what's worse, aren't returning your phone-calls, maybe because they've become tired of you constantly upping the ante. It's also possible that circumstances have changed since last week, and the artist or catalogue being sought after no longer seems as attractive to them. So they walk away.

Of course, there's no scientific method or formula you can use to ascertain if the other side will go an extra mile in your favour or not, no more than there's any way of making the same deduction while playing poker. While you're trying to suss them out, they're doing likewise with you. There's a fine line to be walked between trying to improve an offer one more time and maybe killing the deal stone dead forever. I believe that's where a combination of instinct, knowledge, experience and realism comes in.

Given that we'd begun tentative negotiations in October/November 2013 and the contract wasn't signed until April 2014, there was much too-ing and fro-ing in between with several of the serious contenders. There were three companies with whom I'd accepted general heads of agreement before the real legal work with Sebastian began. Those intensive negotiations took up almost every day of my life from November 2013 right through to April 2014. I made numerous trips to London to meet with all the interested parties who wanted to sign the deal for Hozier/Evolving.

After a particularly tough day of meetings, I recall sitting having a pint in Argyle St in London, opposite the London Palladium (where years previously Clannad had performed). I reflected that when I started out, I couldn't even get into the receptions of the major music companies and now all they were short of doing was laying out the red carpet for me. I found myself humming those famous lines from Van Morrison, 'nobody told me there'd be days like this.' It's a funny old rock'n'roll world indeed!

All major music publishers have business affairs departments which include a number of top-flight lawyers and one of their roles is to produce a more detailed contract that encompasses the heads of agreement that have already been agreed in outline terms.

In relation to the specifics of the contract we eventually signed, I went through aspects of it virtually every day with Sebastian to the point that I nearly knew the document off by heart by the time it was signed. An hour-long phone conversation might revolve around the implications of three short paragraphs and might take place late in the evening after both of us had put in full days at our respective offices. But it had to be done.

The day we signed was one of both relief and excitement. It's exciting because you can start looking forward to your client company growing on a global scale, and the relief comes from the feeling of a job well done and properly concluded to everybody's satisfaction after the deeply intense, complex and mentally exhausting negotiations.

In the end we signed an administration agreement for a specific number of years with Sony/ATV Music for the world *excluding* Ireland. Outsiders might not understand the significance of this, but it meant we were able to keep control of the entire Evolving catalogue from Ireland which meant that ALL potential uses of the songs in the Evolving catalogue had to be cleared by us first.

So not only are we notified about all approaches for uses of our songs, but we have the option to turn down any we felt were unsuitable or the wrong 'fit' for us. This isn't just an issue of money, but it means that a songwriter with, say, strong views on the environment, can refuse to have his or her song used in a TV commercial for a chemical product.

I've been asked if the companies who lose out in such negotiations feel any rancour towards you for not opting to go with them, but to me that would be a surprising reaction from professionals. All the companies who sought the Evolving Music catalogue know how the system works and know there can be only one winner. I can understand they might be disappointed, especially after the time and energy they would've put into the discussions, but I doubt they feel any rancour.

On reflection it was a satisfying experience for me to have negotiated with the top companies, competed at that level and delivered what I believe was an excellent deal for my clients. I also made invaluable contacts and now have the ear of the top guys in the industry and they all know me, and, I hope, would think of me and happily talk to me again if similar circumstances arise.

By the time the music publishing deal was concluded, Hozier's stature had grown. His debut album was released in Ireland in September 2013 to considerable acclaim, and by year's end 'Take Me To Church' had clocked up an extraordinary number of streams and YouTube views and been named by Spotify as one of their ten most viral tracks.

As I mentioned, I'd seen him live for the second time in the Pepper Canister in Mount Street in Dublin in December 2013 where he was scheduled to do two gigs. He'd only recently made his television debut for the *Other Voices* programme recorded in Dingle, Co Kerry, not bad progress for a guy having played a couple of public gigs. The pair of Pepper Canister gigs attracted a horde of music industry insiders, (and I was in the middle of the aforementioned negotiations) and the first of the gigs was beset by power problems. But the second was spot-on, and it was clear the artist had developed a new level of confidence that hadn't been in evidence the first time I'd seen him.

Come February 2014 and record licensing deals were concluded by Rubyworks (our record label to whom Hozier is signed) with Columbia Records for the USA and Canada, and with Universal for the rest of the world.

A concert set for Whelan's in Dublin sold out in 48 seconds, details of his first USA tour were also announced, and Hozier performed on two renowned USA TV shows, the *Late Show with David Letterman* and the *Ellen De Generes show* in May. I could only wonder how long it would've taken an Irish act in the analogue age to get from first recorded release to the Letterman show, whereas Hozier had gone from zero to global musical hero in a mere 10 months!

He was one of the key attractions on the Glastonbury and Longitude festivals, and tracks from the album began to feature in prestigious US television shows such as *The Voice* and *American Idol* throughout the summer months. Adele showed up for his London headliner at Koko in September, and Irish holidaymakers travelling abroad were coming back with tales of the number of times they'd heard Hozier tracks in shops, cafes, restaurants and clubs, as well as on foreign radio and television stations.

Other artists soon started covering his songs, including Ed Sheeran who performed a handsome live version of 'Take Me To Church' on the BBC's *Live Lounge* programme, and when Taylor Swift tweeted about attending one of his shows it prompted another serious boost to his profile. So, by October 2014 Hozier had hit 70 million downloads and his bewildering march to world domination seemed unstoppable.

I saw him again in 2014 at a pre-Christmas live concert in Dublin's Olympia Theatre and found he'd taken another massive leap forward in terms of confidence, stage presence and overall stagecraft. Throughout that show he was constantly hassled by an audience heckler who insisted on shouting stuff at him. Eventually Hozier got tired of this, and although he's not given to publicly uttering profanities, he looked down at the guy from the stage and said, 'You're a real fucking charmer, aren't you?' This brought the house down, as audiences are generally as irritated by persistent hecklers as artists are.

Backstage after the show he and I even joked about his immense improvement stage wise compared to his first tentative performances not so long ago. I was again stuck by how he was the same relaxed, affable guy on or off stage, and how he was honest enough to admit that while he was enjoying the stage shows he was finding the promo stuff, the endless interviews and photo-shoots, to be quite tough. That said I admired how sensibly he was willing to accept that the media work has to be done as it comes as part of the job. That he could take it all in his stride at such a relatively young age is remarkable. We've witnessed mature people who've achieved lower levels of fame and wealth and gone completely off the rails, unable to handle the freedom that fame, success and wealth often bring.

Although I've never thought of rock music and ballet as natural bedfellows, I was very impressed when the Ukraine dancer Sergei Polunin released a video in February 2015 in which he dances to 'Take Me To Church'. Last time I checked it had over 23 million views.

On St Patrick's Day, 2015 I flew over to Nashville, Tennessee to see him perform live at the famous Ryman Auditorium, and when the audience sang Happy Birthday to him (his 25th) during the show it was one of the most emotional feelings I've ever experienced at any gig anywhere. Even for us background people, there's immense satisfaction standing at the back of a venue watching our artists enthral the crowd with their performance knowing we're (a vital) part of the team.

It was also apparent that Denis, Caroline and Andrew had put together a superbly talented band of musicians and a hugely professional crew to really make the live shows sound and look terrific. No doubt this helped to garner the many rave reviews in the international media, including influential music blogs.

The band for the 2014/5 tour was a wonderful mix of Irish and international performers, including Mia Fitzgerald (keyboards), Rory Doyle (drums), Alex Ryan (bass guitar) and Alana Henderson (cello). All of them contributed backing vocals alongside the UK's Lorraine Barnes and the USA's Rachel Lampa.

Jake Ryan was the Tour Manager (who later received a Tour Manager of the Year Award), and he was ably supported by Front Of House Sound Engineer Gavin Muddiman, with Lighting Engineer Matthew Kilmurry, and Murt Murphy on Backline Technician duties. Darren Dunphy was the Monitor Engineer. Sue 'Duchess' Iredale handled production and the logistics of moving the troupe around the world (no mean feat, given the intense schedule that top-flight acts like Hozier have to undertake). When they were later acclaimed as the hardest working band of the year it was reckoned they'd traveled a distance equal to three quarters of the way to the moon!

Immediately after those memorable Nashville shows I noticed that whereas many artists are rushed off by their posse of minders to the privacy of their luxury hotel, Hozier spent a long time chatting and taking selfies with about 200 fans who'd waited patiently at the stage door each night.

After the final Nashville show, we all met up in the Hotel reception. While I was heading off for a flight to meet the Sony/ATV folks in Los Angeles, the band and crew were boarding their sleeper bus to take a 22-hour drive to Dallas. There was certainly no time for partying, no more than there'd been with Celtic Woman or with Clannad before them. I don't know where Hozier and other acts get that strength and dedication from, but they sure have it in spades. The public sometimes think that the music business is very glamorous, but they don't realise the hard work and professionalism it takes to make it to, and stay at, the top.

Another highlight to end that year, was Andrew being nominated for a Grammy Award, and in May 2015 he was presented with an Ivor Novello Song Of The Year Award for 'Take Me To Church'. It's one of the most prestigious awards any songwriter can receive, it's the Oscar's of the music world, and I was delighted to be invited to attend the colourful award ceremony at Grosvenor House Hotel in London. Ever the incurable music fan, I was also pleased to have the opportunity to have my photo taken with Sir Elton John, one of my all-time favourite songwriters. Who says showbiz people are only in it for the money?

2015 Sir Elton John and Hozier, London

Later in the evening, Sony/ATV generously hosted a celebratory party at the world famous Groucho Club in London. I experienced another surreal moment when I was at the bar with the highly-respected Dublin music lawyer Willie Ryan, who also handles legal affairs for Andrew. Right in front of us a club patron was being taught how to play 'Take Me To Church' on the club's piano. Willie and I looked at each and just laughed. Hozier's music was everywhere! Happy days!

The second half of 2015 saw Hozier embark on his first world tour and rack up an enviable list of gold and platinum discs for sales of both the album and single in nearly two dozen countries.

In October 2015 I was invited to the BMI Awards at the Dorchester Hotel in London to accept an award on behalf of Evolving Music. I was asked to make an acceptance speech which, of course, I was delighted to do. I thought it was also an opportunity, in the good old show biz tradition, to poke a little fun at some colleagues, so when it came to say 'I'd like to thank the good people at Sony/ATV', I pretended to read my notes and said 'It says here.' It was just a bit of fun and got a few laughs at their expense. Then I concluded by saying that 'In showbiz we have a saying that you should 'Show up, Show off, and Fuck off.' Which is exactly what I did, ending with a swift 'Thank you.' That earned a few more chuckles too. What a memorable night that was!

2015 BMI Awards Presentation

By the end of the year, Hozier was feted with numerous other awards, including Artist of the Year on VHI, and BBC Song of the Year for 'Take Me To Church'. No doubt that mantelpiece has required several more extensions since then!

But none of this happens by accident. Not only has his success been earned by the groundwork put in by the team in Ireland, led by Caroline and Denis, but by a support network of activists all around the globe. Much of Hozier's success in the USA can be put down to the active support and commitment he received from Columbia Records Chairman and CEO, Rob Stringer. It was Rob who brought Adele to Hozier's London show, and I was delighted to chat with both of them after the gig.

While Rob was an early convert to his potential, Hozier's success also confounded many experienced music industry experts who predicted that one major impact of the digital age would be that we'd never again see acts of the global stature of Michael Jackson, David Bowie or U2. But the staggering worldwide successes of several new artists, including Adele, Ed Sheeran, Taylor Swift, Snow Patrol and Hozier himself, proves how wrong even seasoned veterans can be.

Indeed, by the end of 2015 Hozier generated over 1 billion streams, and that figure was achieved only after something like eighteen months as an international artist! Set that alongside U2 who made their first recording in 1979 but didn't enjoy comparable international success until 1983 with their *War* album and you get some measure of his extraordinary achievement.

To my mind, Hozier displays wisdom beyond his years and he talks perfect sense, not necessarily common in rock and pop stars. Asked by the *New Zealand Herald* if his second album might contain another hit of the calibre of 'Take Me To Church'? He replied, 'I'd rather not be writing songs under pressure for them to be hits, because you're sacrificing what you want to say and the honesty of yourself. If music or art is made with the intention for it to be popular, you're detracting from your own motive, and from yourself.'

That maturity is evident in his lyrics which, when I first read them, blew me away with their insight. In 'Take Me To Church' he sings 'Take me to Church, I'll worship like a dog at the shrine of your lies'. This was written at a time when Ireland was still reeling from a procession of stories about the Catholic clergy's assault and abuse of children that the Church itself actively tried to shield from the law. In those words I feel Hozier captured the anger felt by many Irish people, including staunch Catholics, at the way they'd been lied to and misled. Very few Irish songwriters have been so outspoken about the Catholic Church, and you could spend a day simply reflecting on the implications of the two lines quoted above.

Another of his lyrics that really struck home with me comes in his song 'Jackie Wilson' where he sings 'She blows out of nowhere, a roman candle of the wild, laughing her way through my feeble disguise'. That's amazing stuff for a young man.

Hozier might at times seem quiet and introverted, but he's very determined and courageous when he wants to be, and that honesty comes through very forcefully in the numerous press interviews he's done and even on Irish television when he was interviewed about his religious beliefs by the legendary Irish broadcaster Gay Byrne, on his Irish TV programme *The Meaning Of Life*.

Of course, one of the beauties of music is that lyrics can mean lots of different things to different people, and some can enjoy songs without getting into the detail of the lyrics. But with Hozier it fascinates me that on the outside the songs are so powerful, but when you delve under the surface and into the lyrics there's so much more to discover.

Maybe we shouldn't be too surprised, given that his parents are both creative people. His father John was a respected drummer in blues bands before disability overtook him, and his mother Raine has a BA Honours degree in Visual Arts Practice and actually designed the cover of his debut album. Hozier's brother John is successful in his own right in the film business and made several of his videos.

Perhaps it's that creative environment that gave Hozier the stability that enabled him to keep both feet firmly on the ground, not to mention the general Irish tendency to react against any artist who might be getting notions above their station. It's that approach to people that means you can go into a pub in Ireland and see Bono, or Bruce Springsteen or Joe Elliott sitting with their mates having a pint and a laugh and not a minder in sight. I once saw the actress Goldie Hawn and her partner Kurt Russell sitting having a drink with a couple of friends while watching the St Patrick's Day parade in Dublin, and they seemed as relaxed as could be. Nobody bothered them and that's the way it is in Ireland and I suspect this is one of the reasons international 'stars' like coming here. I don't think you'd see Beyoncé, Justin Bieber, Madonna or Lady Gaga doing likewise in the USA, but that's how it is here, and Hozier fits comfortably into that lifestyle.

As a straight guy he was given much credit for his outspoken support of gay rights. He's actively campaigned for the LGBGT community, especially during the successful Irish same sex marriage referendum as well as taking up the plight of the homeless people in Ireland. In fact, much attention was drawn to the video for 'Take Me To Church' because it contained a scene of two guys kissing and also featured a gay Russian guy being beaten. More recently, he was prominent in the campaign to repeal the Eight Amendment to the Irish constitution as it pertained to abortion issues. Here was a clear example of Hozier being instinctively in touch with the views of the people despite some of the establishment tending to take an opposite, conservative view.

His song 'Cherry Wine' tackles the perennial issue of domestic violence from the male perspective, once again reinforcing his willingness to tackle subjects that others, often prefer to sidestep. In a sense he's been seen by some commentators as a direct link back to the singer-songwriters of the sixties, crusaders of the calibre of Woody Guthrie, Joan Baez, Pete Seeger, Nina Simone and Bob Dylan, who similarly tackled serious social issues that many would've preferred to leave alone.

At the beginning of 2016 he teamed up with the Oscar nominated Irish actress Saoirse Ronan for a video to support the release of a version of 'Cherry Wine' specifically for the campaign highlighting that issue of domestic violence. When it premiered on Valentine's Day I got a few minutes with Saoirse for a chat. I thanked her for supporting the campaign and congratulated her on her Oscar-nomination. I also expressed my admiration for her fine performance in the film *Brooklyn*, making the point that much of it was filmed in the small town of Enniscorthy where I live and where Colm Toibin, author of the book on which the film is based, was born.

Saoirse was as pleasantly natural and affable as Hozier and reminded me that she grew up in a small Irish town, Carlow, not far from Enniscorthy. I believe Saoirse is another major Irish star in the making and is currently being touted as the next Meryl Streep.

Meanwhile the Hozier rise continues. 'Take Me To Church' has by now racked up a mind-boggling 230 million YouTube hits, quite a far cry from the very early days when Colette and myself would do a daily check on it and wonder if it'd ever reach the 'magic' figure of 1 million!

Andrew toured the world up to March 2016 when he decided to take a break and write some new songs. He'd been on the road solidly for the best part of three years.

Many people have asked me why, apart from 'Better Love' (a track from the movie *The Legend of Tarzan*), he hasn't released any new work in the ensuing three years.

Consider this: all songwriters/performers have their whole lives to write their first record, (as we in the biz refer to CDs or LPs) and draw on the songs they've spent all that time writing.

The second record, which we call, 'that second difficult album', can be far harder to write. Obviously, the songsmith is trying to improve their previous work, and this can cause many to delay the release of their follow up recording.

Hozier has just announced that he will begin a new tour in the USA in the fall of 2018 which will also include new songs. I, for one, am looking forward to seeing him live and hearing his new work. I believe Andrew Hozier Byrne is a major talent whose work will last for hundreds of years hence. Only time will tell, folks. Time will tell.

AFTERWORD

When in 2016 I became an Old Age Publisher (OAP) I decided to take stock of my life. I said to myself 'Johnny man, you're runnin' out of real estate'. Who knows how long we'll all live?

I've suffered all my life with Dyslexia and just can't spell for toffee. It's common enough in the creative community and many articles have been written about this phenomenon. It's never been a hindrance for me, but rather a life-long inconvenience. It's bonkers; I can do complicated calculations in my head with numbers and percentages, but don't ask me to spell the simplest of words!

I joined my first band in 1964 and had, in reality, been performing (I use that term rather loosely!), managing, publishing, or one of the many other jobs I'd done (sound engineer, lighting engineer, roadie, publicity person, music lecturer, etc.) for all those years. I achieved a lot, from being involved in bringing Clannad to the world stage to overseeing the publishing affairs for Hozier's worldwide hit, 'Take Me To Church' which reached the top twenty in over 40 countries around the world. I recently concluded a consultation with Picture This, an exciting new band from Athy just starting out on their career. They already played a gig in Dublin in June 2018 which sold 35,000 tickets and just headlined Electric Picnic 2018!

2016 with Picture This at their first ever gig in Dublin

On my 66th birthday, I found myself in London attending a showcase gig for Otherkin who've been described as a 'four-piece punky new-wave pop band'. Two of the guys are actually qualified doctors who'd passed on the medical profession, in order to have a go at a career in music. I was talking to the frontman and singer Luke Reilly, one of the aforementioned medics. I'd seen their high energy (brilliant) set many times and knowing what was to come, I said to Luke 'I'll be in the mosh pit* and if I go down, please DO NOT RESUSCITATE'. They laughed. I said 'Guys, do you know how long I've been rockin' it out? … I shocked myself when I did the math and worked out the answer which was 52 years!

I've always believed that when the time is right, you have to get off the stage and, if possible, do so at the height of your career. I'd reached the zenith of the goals I'd set myself. So, on 19th August 2016 I resigned my position as administrator of The Evolving Music Company Ltd and informed Dave Kavanagh that I'd retire from Liffey Publishing Ltd and all the other companies we'd formed over the years, at the end of 2016. In the event, that didn't happen until mid-2017. Little did I know that Dave himself would leave us in early 2018.

2016 Otherkin wrap party

I have no definite plan as to what's next in my life, but whatever time I have left on the planet, I'm determined to enjoy it and try and concentrate on my health and live as stress free as possible. I still have many business interests. I'm involved, as an advisor director, in a 'Start Up' business in the tech sector locally in Wexford, I remain a Board member of IMRO, MCPS (Ire) Ltd and the Music Publishers Association in Ireland (MPAI) and am in the process of forming a JV* music publishing company.

As I write it's 2018 and Ireland is experiencing the hottest summer in years. (Someone should really speak to DumpleTrump about Climate Change!). Hozier is about to release new music and starts touring in the USA in September. I'm really excited about that, as I believe he is a tremendous talent and will turn out to be a legend of the Irish music biz.

Enniscorthy, Co Wexford is on the main international flight path between the West and East. I have an App on my IPhone called 'Plane Finder'. I often sit out on my deck looking over the town and the Slaney River, then look up and think to myself 'Look at all those planes flying between New York and London, and me not in them'. Been there, done that and have a drawer full of the tee shirts!!

Who can tell what the coming years, or even the coming weeks will bring to 'the business they call show'. I read all the blogs, updates, and legal changes daily. All I can say at this stage is that I'm alive, healthy, & enjoying my 'retirement' but alert to any changes and challenges that might be coming around the bend, while at the same time looking back with gratitude for the opportunity to work for over 40 years in the industry and marvel at what a genuinely wonderful trip it's been.

I was at a party one night in a room full of top international songwriters and Shay Healy, the writer of several hit songs, introduced me to the room as follows, 'This is Johnny Lappin, a man who has been in the right place at the right time – TWICE.'

In the immortal words of one of my favourite songs by Joe Walsh, 'Life's Been Good'...... So Far.

2014 Hozier's First Gold Disc with Niall Muckian, Rubyworks Records

2016 with the High Kings

EPILOGUE

During the post-Stepaside period while I was managing Time Machine, I was walking along by Trinity College when I was tapped on the shoulder by this small young teenage chap who said to me, 'Excuse me, is your name Johnny Lappin?'

When I admitted I was, he said, 'My name is Paul Hewson, but everybody calls me Bono Vox. I'm in a band called U2.'

I looked at him in my typically arrogant way and said, 'Yeah. So?'

He said, 'You manage a band called Time Machine and they're playing in the Baggot Inn next week.'

'Yes', I said impatiently, 'What of it?'

And Bono said, 'We were wondering if there's any chance U2 could do the support slot?'

I looked at him quite dismissively and said, 'Look, son, why don't you send a demo tape into my office?'

He never did.

But Hey ...... You can't win 'em all!!

2017 Self with U2's Edge

ACKNOWLEDGEMENTS

Writing a book like this is hard, especially when the author is dyslexic and is not a natural born writer. At the beginning of the process, it feels like a daunting task. Initially, there's the self-doubt that anyone would have the slightest interest in reading about another person's life. After all, we each have our own experiences and stories to tell. In the music industry, the performers and artists are sometimes known as the 'front of house' people that the public come to see or hear. That old showbiz expression or idiom that they're lured by 'the smell of the greasepaint and the roar of the crowd' and so, the stage is their domain. It's a tough career to take on, because I reckon the failure rate is close to ninety percent, if not higher. Then, there are the 'background people' like myself, managers, advisors, agents, drivers, publicists, road crews, stagehands, engineers and a myriad of other folk who the public don't normally see or even know about. Their role is one of being a support mechanism to the other side. Any successful performer will tell you that having a good 'team' around them is vital, whereas many unsuccessful 'Artists' will often blame them for their failure. Strangely, or perhaps not, many people, including myself, who end up in this supporting 'cast' started out as performers themselves, and having failed, decide to stay on in the entertainment business in some guise or another. Showbiz is indeed a strange calling, but as the fella said, it beats working!!

The music biz has been kind to me. I've travelled the world in it and managed to make a reasonable living from it. Despite all the madness and parties, somehow, I've managed to stay reasonably healthy and, *apparently,* I'm still alive!

They say in a lifetime you meet about 80,000 people and I guess I've nearly met my quota, however in composing this tome, there are people without whom etc etc …

Clare Keogh: For her 24/7 bubbly enthusiasm, encouragement, guidance and for convincing me I was a writer . . . . . Am I?

VixenCR3: Grammar Gaffer, Spellchecker, 'Covert' Comforter and A Woman of Most Importance!

Jackie Hayden: The 'Heritage' Hack with the quick quip for his knowledge, assistance and countless hours of listening to me rabbiting on . . . . .

Ibar Carty: Snapper Supremo under blindingly cross-eyed pressure and for his tips on 'How To Be A Poseur'!

Board Colleagues: To all my colleagues on the Boards of IMRO, MCPS and MPAI for the conversations, conundrums and healthy debates over all the years. I've sat at many tables with them, but they've never managed to drink me under one!

Morgan Farrell: My local 'Red Liner' buddy with the 'sweet' tooth, for his friendship and thoughtful observations.

To all my family, friends and acquaintances, far too many to mention individually . . . .

The Fox Is Outta The Covert!!

THE JARGON

A&R
This stands for Artist & Repertoire. These folks are the people who are sent out from Record (and Publishing) Companies to seek out new talent.

BRILL BUILDING
The legendary songwriting building on Broadway, New York City where many hit songs were born. The building also housed many music publishing companies who would vie to sign the best of the songwriters' works.

COVER SONG
This refers to a song written by one party and performed by another party. For example, bands that play other people's songs are known as 'Cover Bands'

J.V.
This stands for Joint Venture, where individuals or companies form a type of partnership arrangement for a specific purpose or project.

LICENSING
A single process where one party licenses another party for specific territories i.e. an Irish record label may license a record for another territory such as the USA.

LIGGER

An individual who attends parties, openings, record launches etc with the intention of schmoozing with the 'insiders' to promote either themselves or their clients' wares.

MOSH PIT

The area immediately in front of the stage, where enthusiastic fans get as close to the band as they possibly can. Not for the faint-hearted or those with a nervous disposition. Great fun though!

PAYOLA

Rife in the early days of radio. This term was used to christen the practice of paying or bribing a DJ to play records. Thankfully no long common!

PRODUCER

In music terms a producer is the person responsible for the final 'mix' of a record. Highly talented and named producers can command substantial fees per track that they work on. Producer also refers to the person who finances a specific production.

ROADIE

Most people will be familiar with this term. These are the folks that keep the live shows on the road by getting equipment from one venue to the next. A good Roadie is worth his weight in gold!

SUB-PUBLISHING

A sub-publisher acts as an agent on behalf of the original publisher, that is to represent the catalogue in a particular territory for a specific term.

SYNCHRONISATION RIGHTS

Sync' Rights refer to the right to use a piece of music with some king of visual image such as is used in film, TV, advertisements, video games etc.

TOUR MANAGERS

These are the hard working folks who look after bands when they're on the road. Last to bed and first to rise aptly described by the legendary TM Paddy McPoland (High Kings) on his twitter handle as:

'Global Executive Baby-Sitting Services for Adults.'

Well put Paddy!

A poem I picked up in an antique shop in 1971, I love the sentiments expressed in the work. I'm still working on the 'Go placidly' bit!

DESIDERATA

GO PLACIDLY AMID THE NOISE & HASTE, & REMEMBER WHAT PEACE THERE MAY BE IN SILENCE. AS FAR AS POSSIBLE WITHOUT surrender be on good terms with all persons. Speak your truth quietly & clearly; and listen to others, even the dull & ignorant; they too have their story. 🙟 Avoid loud & aggressive persons, they are vexations to the spirit. If you compare yourself with others, you may become vain & bitter; for always there will be greater & lesser persons than yourself. Enjoy your achievements as well as your plans. 🙟 Keep interested in your own career, however humble; it is a real possession in the changing fortunes of time. Exercise caution in your business affairs; for the world is full of trickery. But let this not blind you to what virtue there is; many persons strive for high ideals; and everywhere life is full of heroism. 🙟 Be yourself. Especially, do not feign affection. Neither be cynical about love; for in the face of all aridity & disenchantment it is perennial as the grass. 🙟 Take kindly the counsel of the years, gracefully surrendering the things of youth. Nurture strength of spirit to shield you in sudden misfortune. But do not distress yourself with imaginings. Many fears are born of fatigue & loneliness. Beyond a wholesome discipline, be gentle with yourself. 🙟 You are a child of the universe, no less than the trees & the stars; you have a right to be here. And whether or not it is clear to you, no doubt the universe is unfolding as it should. 🙟 Therefore be at peace with God, whatever you conceive Him to be, and whatever your labors & aspirations, in the noisy confusion of life keep peace with your soul. 🙟 With all its sham, drudgery & broken dreams, it is still a beautiful world. Be careful. Strive to be happy. 🙟 🙟

FOUND IN OLD SAINT PAUL'S CHURCH, BALTIMORE; DATED 1692

For

Suzanne,Jonathan, Rosie, Adriana, Andrew, Liria, Stephen, Christiany

24133390R00130

Printed in Great Britain
by Amazon